AFRICAN RHYTHMS

-

New Approaches to Literature

Smith and Ce [ed.]

AFRICAN
Library of Critical Writing

AFRICAN RHYTHMS –New Approaches to Literature
Smith and Ce (Ed.)

©African Library of Critical Writing
Print Edition
ISBN: 978-9-7837-0859-4

For information address:
Progeny (Press) International
Email: progeny.int@gmail.com
For: African Books Network
9 Handel Str.
AI EBS 480001 NG WA
Email: handelbook@gmail.com

Marketing and Distribution in the US, UK,
Europe, N. America (Canada),
and Commonwealth countries by

African Books Collective Ltd.
PO Box 721
Oxford OX1 9EN
United Kingdom
Email: orders@africanbookscollective.com

j

Contents

Introduction

AFRICAN Rhythms has come on a timely note with new integrative and indigenous approaches to literary affairs in spite of the cultural myopia of some western critics. Here, the so-called minority nations may yet become major estuaries in the global sea. The imaginative approach to Africa's development issues being the cardinal point of council research formations therefore informed selections for the primary edition of these series from our African Library of Critical Writing.

Once again the onus is on critics to turn the searchlight on African thought and oratorical strategies of aesthetic communion. With very many approaches, it was important that a great deal of this part dwelt on the question of traditional influences. But this is no less surprising in itself. Recall that early recognition accorded writings from the continent had come from the efforts of leading writers like Chinua Achebe on whose works the contribution of two scholars had proffered an illuminating insight from outside Africa. Two subsequent chapters follow this pattern to assess the work of literature which, by fusing traditional elements in transitional societies, illustrate the cultural awareness that touches upon the exalted role of the artiste in his community. It is their argument that both old and new works of prose fiction adopt oratorical strategies of African literary education either in order to reaffirm some of Africa's positive traditions or critique changing behavioural traits that corrode traditional ethos and impinge on genuine development of society.

The growing concern about African youth development is at the heart of the dialogue with internationally acknowledged children's fiction writer Anezi Okoro. Similarly, on the subject of child heroes in Africa, we have written about two examples in African fiction showing convergence of vision in Ngugi wa Thiongo and Ferdinand Oyono on Africa's colonial experience.

The post colonial rhetoric continues with echoes of political commitment –twin issues in the African discourse and our writer explores this growing phenomenon in the poetry of one member of the younger generation of Nigerian writers.

Probably the highpoint of this edition of African literature has been the overarching signification of the folk literatures of Africa in a manner of cultural celebration often taken by the West as belonging in the past. Two scholars of African orature have written respectively on the birth songs of Cameroonian women performers and the riddle contests of youth artistes from Nigeria in a manner that recognises the immediate relevance of this greatly cherished but neglected part of African literary aesthetics.

In spite of all exuberance, however, the collections in this edition may only whet the appetite for the imaginative chronicle of Africa's literary progress in the last decade.

-C S and C C

Chapter 1

Oratorical Strategies in African Literature

Sone and Toko

Tradition and African Literature

Traditional literature in Africa (orature) serves as an instrument for examination of individual experience in relation to the normative order of society. It was used, and is still being used in several parts of rural Africa to chart social progress or to comment on how society adheres to or deviates from general community aesthetic. Seen in this light, traditional literature as a creation of the imagination ultimately derives its material from the realities of society. As mirror of the society it enables the community to teach, entertain, and explore the ambiguities of human existence. The substance of human experience out of which orature is created is that which has made sufficient impact in the community to excite the imagination of the people to literary creativity. One of these experiences is civic responsibility and leadership training which is sadly lost in modernised or postcolonial environment.

Quite often in traditional literature characters are classified in three categories –heroes, antiheroes and villains. Effective leadership is usually entrusted in the hands of a heroic character. The hero is one who finds personal satisfaction in the service of his community or one who has offered invaluable services to the community. Of course, there may be monarchies and dynasties with their autocrats, dictators and despots. But the leader, where there was one, was somebody who must submerge his private interests in the pursuit of national ideals which were also in harmony with universal morality. The point we intend to make is that the ideals of good leadership are fundamental to the concerns of African oratory. African folk tales reveal three broad attitudes of communal attitudes towards leadership and social change as reflected in the three tales we have selected for study below.

Tale No. 1 Tortoise The Wise

In Tale Number One1 from the North West Province, tortoise rogue and wheeler-dealer wisely accepts the authority of the lion. One day, lion, goat and tortoise go on a hunting expedition at the end of which they kill a deer. The meat is brought to the home of the lion for sharing. Lion calls on the goat to share the meat. Goat, on its part, decides to share the meat into three equal parts. Lion is angry that goat has treated him as an ordinary citizen rather than a king and therefore strikes goat with such force that he dies. Lion then turns to tortoise and asks him to proceed with the sharing of the meat. Tortoise divides the meat into two parts-one very large and the other very small. He gives the large part to the lion and keeps the small one for himself. Lion is happy with the "wisdom" of tortoise and asks him where he learnt how to share meat so well.

Tortoise points at the dead goat and replies, "by looking at my dead companion".

The lion in the above tale represents the benevolent despot who will do everything to ensure that his personal interest is served first and his authority is enforced very strongly. It is obvious that the lion will want to see the status quo maintained and entrenched so that he can continue to exploit and oppress the masses unchallenged. While the lion's aversion to change is motivated by greed, tortoise's conservation is caused by fear. Tortoise here represents the majority of Africans who are disgusted with their self-seeking leaders but at the same time will do nothing concrete to remove them from power for fear of the attendant consequences. It is common for this group of socio-passive Africans to point at social stability by focusing upon peace, order, continuity and regularity as basis for their being conformist. They also argue that since the outcome of political innovation cannot be predicted with absolute certainty, it follows, logically that the known ways should be preferred to the unknown. Put differently, "Whatever is, good, however imperfect it may be". Nevertheless, such resistance to political change based on the refusal to share, contradicts the fundamental principle of collective responsibility in traditional African society.

Tale No. 2. "How Vulture Turned Scavenger"

Tale Number Two2 from Garoua in the North province of Cameroon is essentially about the use of force to overthrow tyranny thus:

Once upon a time, all birds of the sky assembled to discuss on how to depose vulture, their leader-turned-despot. Parrot, their spokesman stepped forward to address them. He began by thanking them for answering his call. He then went into the heart of the matter. He said: "It is now seven years since we gathered here and unanimously elected vulture as our chief. At that time, we all thought that vulture could protect us and take care of our interests better than hawk. That was why we chose him. But, since then, vulture has proved to us that the reverse is true. He does not dialogue with us any more. Rather he prefers to maintain an imperial distance from us. He taxes us arbitrarily and seizes our properties with impunity. Whenever any of us raises his voice in protest, he is visited that very night by the owls, his dreaded secret police. I say enough is enough. Vulture must go." Sparrow took the floor and said, "Parrot has spoken very well. We all agree that vulture must go. The question is, how?"

Crow cut in and said, "Where there is a will, there is a way. Vulture may be powerful, he may have bat as his spy and the owls as his secret police. But they cannot fight all of us if we stand as a group. Therefore let us all march to the palace and drive vulture away".

So all the birds marched to the palace. With no Bat to warn him of the approaching danger, vulture was taken completely by surprise and had to run away to the desert where he now lives on carrion away from the other birds.

Although this is an aetiological tale meant to explain why the vulture scavenges, it can be used to illustrate the use of violence to overthrow tyranny. It is to be noted here that the birds did not use violence for its own sake. Rather they resorted to it when all other peaceful means have proved ineffective. In their reaction, the birds represent the group of political activists who reject the status quo because it has thwarted their expectations.

The necessity of violence as a means of expressing and achieving political preferences has been emphasized in struggles for liberty throughout the world. In fact, most of the great political changes the world has known have taken place under violent conditions. African traditions while acknowledging the fact that violence may pay off where other means have failed, are constrained to reject coercive, costly and disruptive actions whose results are uncertain.

Tale No. 3. "Tortoise Rides the Elephant"

Between the two extremes of the political spectrum discussed above is an intermediary group of Africans who encourage political change provided it is brought about peacefully. This is reflected in tale Number Three3 from the Bakossi of Kupe Muanenguba Division in the South West Province of Cameroon.

Elephant was always boasting that he is the biggest animal and, therefore, the king of the forest. Tortoise, on his part, countered by saying that kingship depended not on size but on wisdom and since he was reputed to be the wisest animal, it followed, naturally that he was king of all animals.

Elephant could not understand why his authority should be challenged by such a nonentity as tortoise so he put the case before the other animals. A date was fixed for the hearing and the elephant waited anxiously for the day so that the question of his authority would be resolved once and for all.

On the day of the hearing, all the animals assembled at the market place. Elephant paraded majestically waiting for the decision to be taken. But the hearing could not begin because tortoise was absent. Enquiries were made about his whereabouts but no animal seemed to know anything. At last, lizard ventured to say that on his way to the market place that morning, he passed through tortoise's house and found him to be in bed writhing with pain. When he asked what was wrong, tortoise told him that he had fallen down a palm-tree that morning and broken a leg. As a result he was unable to attend the hearing on foot. When elephant heard that, he offered to go personally to bring tortoise. But when tortoise saw elephant coming he knew immediately that his trick had worked. The great elephant had fallen into his trap!

Elephant told tortoise that he heard of the accident, and offered to come and carry him to the market place. Tortoise thanked him and pleaded with him to be gentle as he was in great pain. Elephant agreed. He carried tortoise and moved gently. But, as soon as they got near the market place, tortoise began to act like a royalty and made as if he was giving orders to the elephant. The elephant reached the market place and carefully stooped for the tortoise who now descend in majesty. He was hailed by all as king. When Elephant realised what had happened he became quite furious. But it was too late. Tortoise had been acknowledged king.

Of particular importance is that Tortoise had used his intelligence, and not brute force, to carry out the most successful coup d'etat against the elephant. The emphasis here is on the universality of intelligence which is the basis of equality among men and the justification for democracy as a political system.

Modern Oratorical Teaching Strategies: The Dark Child *and* Children of Koloko

16

Salient methods of African education through orature are evident in Laye Camara's The Dark Child and Chin Ce's Children of Koloko. For instance both novels employ oratorical devices which include songs, legends, proverbs (or the dereliction of them) and folktales for their traditional, as against modern western, teaching strategies.

Harold Courlander notes quite rightly in A Treasury of African Folklore that the traditional African story teller employs myths, traditions, legends, proverbs and wise sayings to "(en)capsulate… the learnings of centuries about the human character and about the intricate balance between people and the world around them (1). This oratorical strategy thus equips the African mind with a sense of orientation that situates him in time and space as it bridges the past, the present and the future. It teaches morals through its unfailing discernment of wrong and right and enables the African child to be anchored to his/her traditions. At the same time, it ploughs the field for his/ her adjustment to the present and future. In this light, Maxwell Okolie is therefore correct in his observation that

> One of the greatest implications of childhood in African literature is not its role as a means of recalling the grandeur and valour that characterized the African peoples' past, but as a period of initiation of the child into the mysteries of nature and existence. (32)

Initiating the child into the mysteries of nature means bringing the child in contact with vegetation, animals, rivers, etc. (the physical nature) as well as making the trainee learn the valuable moral and spiritual values as can be seen in Laye and Yoyo the protagonists of The Dark Child and Children of Koloko respectively. At first both are quite in contact with nature at their Tindican and Boko homes until the time comes for a change of environment that impacts heavily in their consciousness. Earlier the hero of The Dark Child had been involved in farming and thus he is familiar with small game: hares, wild boars, monkeys and birds. Even in the town of Kouroussa, he is shown the father's small snake. Likewise Yoyo in Children of Koloko enjoys the wonders of the natural world at Boko. Nature – fauna and flora– thus represents the first stage of the African child's education in his home environment.

The second phase is achieved by the use of tales, songs, legends, and proverbs. The protagonist of The Dark Child is told stories by his youngest uncle:

> Then it was that my uncle told me how the monkey had tricked the panther who was all ready to eat him, how the palm tree rat had kept the hyena waiting all night for nothing. These were stories I had already heard a hundred times, but I always enjoyed them and laughed so loudly that the wild fowl ahead of us took flight. (46)

In Koloko too, De Tuma is seen at the village meeting "telling a story of olden days when people showed befitting examples of themselves." At the end of his story, he admonishes his listeners thus: "'go and look at yourselves again because it is from your homes that we can guard our brood from the threat of the hawks" (96). After De Tuma's story, Bap tells the audience the tale of father tortoise who had brought home a beautiful maid and had forbidden his sons and all the men folk to touch even a hair of her body.

18

But when the woman becomes pregnant, it was discovered that father tortoise himself had broken his own rule (103).

If all the tales above-mentioned entertain the listeners and readers, their main purpose is to teach principles of leadership and civic responsibility. The recurrent animal imagery used in the tales reveals knowledge of various artistic techniques and shades of meanings. In the first tale, the monkey and the rat are the weak victims that outwit the strong but wicked panther and hyena that stand for the oppressors. De Tuma's mention of hawks illustrates the elders' failure to protect their young ones against danger, while Foreman Obeku's story points at father tortoise who having violated his own law sets a bad example to his sons. His reply to his sons: "All is well my boys; follow my words but not my deeds" is a proof of his inability to teach by personal example, a key principle in African pedagogy. To show public deviation from traditional wisdom in the Koloko stories, proverbs –the device used in teaching morality – are scarce and when used, seem to deviate from this primary role and function. Fathead's talk during the house warming ceremony is stilted:

> Koloko mma-mma-o! I salute you all. Our elders say that gbata gbata is a language that has two faces. It might mean good or it might mean disaster. (131)

and aims at making the masses covet his achievements in building a Magnificent Multi Million Mansion. His second proverb is also a razzle-dazzle allurement:

> I was building this edifice, I had planned how my own people may enjoy the first opening ceremony after which shall come my friends, ministers and

19

fellow directors-general from the capital. For we say it is from the home front that all training must take off. The Englishman says it in another way: "Charity begins at home." (131)

Like in the first statement, the chief misappropriates a traditional saying to fool the masses who already have failed as clairvoyant social critics. Unlike Yoyo they cannot lampoon a crafty, egocentric businessman who squanders money that can improve the whole community's standards of living. As Amanda points out, "in this drama of social and communal acquiescence, tradition is made culprit" (17). The women's songs and the applause are therefore testaments to the adulteration of both tradition and the honourable role of the griot in the traditional African communities.

> The millionaire cometh
> See the millionaire cometh
> All eyes have seen him and
> They say the millionaire cometh!!! (133)

Thus the women, like Billy-Joe Okonofa (Okon for short) and Adede, subject their art to Fathead's millions. Their roles as educators (the griot or king's jester was an educator in traditional African societies) become questionable. Fathead's jesters' song contrasts that of the true griot who sings the douga in The Dark Child:

> He [the praise-singer] was a man who created his song out of some deep inner necessity...He would begin to intone the douga, the great chant which is sung only for celebrated men and which is danced

for them alone. But the douga is a formidable chant, a provocative chant, a chant which the praise-singer dared not sing, and which the man for whom it is sung dared not dance before certain precautions had been taken. (39)

This sacred douga is sung for men like Camara's father who is a man of principles (27). As a goldsmith, he observes the rules of his profession; as a man, he is possessed of high dignity in thought and deed. He is not a millionaire like Fathead in Ce's novel yet he is rich and celebrated because his richness is founded on sound perennial values. Both the griot and the father cannot transgress the moral demands of the douga; they thus preserve the moralizing function that it has always fulfilled in pre-capitalist Africa. In Koloko only the song of Old Bap parallels this chant.

Old Bap's song preserves the morality that underlies both the griot's chants and the Christian songs. In his homage to his grandfather who had outlived and surpassed "any of his peers in all the villages" (171), Yoyo, unlike Fathead's western mediaeval-type court jesters, pays tribute to a poor man who lived according to time old principles of righteousness and human dignity. One of these principles is compassion as seen in his song:

> Who say that my Lord hath
> never given compassion?
> Is there a-ny one my lord hath
> Never given compassion? (172)

Although a hybrid of Christian and traditional lyric, the song which teaches acceptance and forbearance, denotes

African communal ethic of solidarity and "collective responsibility [that] is the very essence of ancestral authority". These principles have been taught Yoyo through this chant, and become the unbreakable link between the grandson and his late grandfather:

> Time was when you sang your song in the loneliness of your nights, your song of consolation which had become the strap by which I shall always remember you. (172)

Thus the song that summarizes Old Bap's life is the bridge between the past, present and future. It is this very tune, reflecting Old Bap's sense of communal responsibility and compassion, which spurs Yoyo's epiphany and attainment of growth. The oratorical strategy of the story can therefore be perceived in "transformative" terms showing us Yoyo's development from immaturity to greater awareness after a psychological crisis. The rising action reaches a peak with Yoyo's epiphanic experience at the northern Trium Press. It later falls with the protagonist's resolution to hold a new attitude (Dora's attitude) "for these sons and daughters of Koloko" (177).

Traditional Teaching versus Western Pedagogy

If genuine traditional teaching strategy uses orature as the main teaching tool, modern western pedagogy in both novels by Camara and Ce is conversely associated with the cane, the blackboard, exercise-book, fountain pen, book (reading), the transistor and newspaper (journalism). Camara's first days at school were saddened by thrashing administered by the teacher and the school bullies until the day his father beat the school director. To the young boy, the blackboard was a nightmare as he notes: "We wanted to be noticed as little as possible, for we lived in continual dread of being sent to the blackboard" (DC 81-82). In this case the school adds a corollary of fear while the exercise-book and fountain pen shown to the child during the circumcision ceremony stand as a challenge to the caste system. Similarly we see Da Kata in Koloko questioning the rationale of reading that cannot provide her with money: "But when will all this book reading end? Won't you get a job and start bringing us money?" Yoyo replies that reading wasn't all about getting a lucrative job these days. (COK 41). When it was first introduced to Africa, the western schooling became synonymous with erudition and monetary acquisition. Learned elite had to be given an office job that ensured a monthly salary. This explains why the old lady cannot understand why her nephew tells her that "reading wasn't all about getting a lucrative job these days".

It is not just reading that is emblematic of the flaws of western pedagogy; its means of communication, the transistor and the press, are also deficient. When Yoyo's mother hears the town crier's "gong-a-gong-a-gong! gong-a-gong-a-gong! gong-a-gong-a-gong!", she summons her grandson: 'Put off that radie and let's know the matter! Put off that noise, I said'" (94). The woman shows her preference for the town crier's message and her grandson is forced to put off the radio/ transistor that announces an estranged government's billion naira budget. The town crier's job is a traditional means of communication that is handed over from one generation to the other (from ageing Long John to young Ham in this case). It therefore guarantees the continuity and stability of traditional life ways which is lacking in the politics of modern Africa. Where Da Kata and Big Mam criticize the book and the radio, Yoyo also castigates the press that teaches lies to young interns. Chief Bada Babatunde, the proprietor of Koloko Herald, who served Dogomutun (Dogkiller) in a servile manner when the latter was still in power, now, uses its news organ to slander his former master. Note the hero's conclusion:

> It made me upset. Not because of everything said about him [Dogkiller] but for the reason that lies were potent weapons- weapons known to politicians, lawyers, policemen, press men and, Dickie would add, preachers. (162)

The local Koloko Herald and Fathead's jesters serve monetary gratification to the detriment of truth. They thus empower unreliable men who only have the executive, judicial or military powers that further alienate the masses.

Conclusion

The comparison of traditional African teaching strategies and those utilized by western culture in the two novels clearly brings out the important place of African folklore in public education. It teaches younger members of the community adherence to social norms, validates social institutions and religious rituals, which all safeguard the sustainability of the best of African traditions and culture.

Before concluding this chapter, it is necessary to comment on the present state of leadership and democracy in Africa which makes this study of orature and its teaching strategies of deep significance for modern African literary and cultural studies. There seems to be the consensus among many concerned individuals and organisations that the political party structures in several African countries have ceased to promote the cause of human liberty and have degenerated into mono-ethnic power monopolies which merely tyrannise the masses, hence the majority of Africans are experiencing profound dissatisfactions engendered by what they perceive as the growing gap between expectation and reality. These dissatisfactions in turn, lead to demands for greater adaptation, innovation and, therefore, change. As the United States Assistant Secretary of State Herman Cohen once remarked:

> Like people everywhere, Africans want and need freedom. And they want what the one-party model has so singularly failed to provide...government based on the equality of all groups rather than dominance by or favouritism toward one; leaders interested in national development rather than the limited perspectives of patronage politics, economic policies that promote rather than preclude individual enterprise.4

The general expectation for Africa today is structural political changes which, hopefully, would replace the one-party with truly pluralistic structures. This preference for a truly multi-party democracy has, to a large extent, been based on the assumption that pluralistic political structures by their very nature, favour "ethnic balance, coalition and compromise". The implication here is that democracy is a system of great adaptability. Seen from this standpoint, it becomes not only necessary but also imperative to reassess continually the democratic reform that has swept through the African continent.

From the oral tales of Africa we have seen three possibilities for political action in Africa which may range from passive obedience through the conventional protest to the ultimate revolution. These three attitudes to political change are however, likely to be more complementary than conflicting perhaps because political change is basically multi-faceted.

Unfortunately the very people who suffer most from oppression and exploitation are also the very ones with the least opportunities and resources to carry out meaningful political change or create political convulsions. In their attempts to reinstate the institutions and values on which democracy is founded and equally rekindle the lights of individual freedom, African writers and activists have, of necessity, joined ranks in articulating the African vision of true democracy and good governance from their own orature and ancient traditions. It is therefore in this bid to bring about genuine transformation of the nation states that African writers teach some basic lessons from their past through the medium of their orature. They recognise that although traditional African societies were often small, close-knit and homogeneous, and so it was consequently easy to practice democracy and good governance on a small scale, there lies a glaring difference with the situation today where most modern African countries are a veritable mosaic of peoples and cultures. Thus they argue that modern African environment can learn at least the rudiments of good governance and democracy from their orature.

We too have sought to demonstrate that the novels *The Dark Child* and *Children of Koloko* are proof of this effort by African writers toward effective education of the young, starting from the trainee's mastery of the natural environment and cultural values. Camara Laye's and Ce's protagonists are able to show precocious or prodigious talents in the midst of a general lack of direction because of their affinity and deference for nature (vegetation, rivers, animals etc.), through their ritualistic journeys, and their exposure to the strategies of African folkloric or oratorical education.

Chapter 2

Oral Rhythms of Achebe's Fiction

Roy and Kirpal

IT is agreed that the phase-shift from speech to writing, from the spoken to the written word was not merely a technical change for it signalled a major transition in modes of perception. But samples of African writing in English appear to indicate that oral modes can survive despite the adoption of the written medium in literature. It will be shown here how Chinua Achebe employs the written form to present an oral culture.[1]

Achebe's reconstruction of Igbo history, his evocation of a traditional culture with a predominantly oral sensibility- a structure of feeling that is still extent in contemporary Nigeria- paradoxically makes use of writing. His books are among the first few written documents on the Igbos. Gareth Griffiths has considered this act, the transmission of an oral culture through writing, as evidence of the writer's participate in the process of the destruction of that pre-literate world.[2] But, given the survival of oral modes of perception in Nigeria in spite of the undermining effects of literacy,[3] it is possible to view

Achebe's *Things Fall Apart* and *Arrow of God* as 'oral' records of Igbo life.

The novels *No Longer at Ease* and *A Man of the People* do not function in the Igbo narrative tradition as explicitly. But they too conceal strikingly oral patterns and habits in their linguistic structures.

The legends of Okonkwo and Ezeulu, of Umuofia and Umuaro, are recounted by the oral teller of tales whose conception of history is very different from ours. For he takes into account not only what has happened but also what is fabled to have happened. He re-constructs the history of his people largely by drawing on myth and legend. While the unlettered artist has the freedom to distort historical facts if necessary, [4]

Achebe is painstakingly accurate and precise in recording the colonial penetration into the bush land. Despite there being absolute fidelity to historical truth, the colonial experience is presented from the perspective of the Igbos. The Igbo voice of the novels perceives and re-creates this experience in the language of myth and legend.

Oral forms, including myth and legend, draw heavily on the repertoire of communal, traditional formulae.[5] A passage in *Things Fall Apart*[6] begins thus:

> That was many years ago, twenty years or more, and during this time Okonkwo's farm had grown like a bush-fire in the harmattan. (p. 3)

This is a phrase- 'many years ago' (the familiar opening of folktales and myths)- which occurs several times in the course of the novel and underlines the tendency to hark back to the past in order to clarify a present event, 'many years ago' reinforces the impression of a vague, indeterminate past in the manner of tales. The explanation, 'twenty years or more', indicates only an approximate rather than a precise number of years because, unlike modern man with his obsession for the minute segmentation of time, the unlettered man, makes only broad divisions to mark time. The his ton' of the tribe is reconstructed not by naming and identifying dates and years but in relation to the phenomena and events that have significantly affected communal life.[7]

> The year that Okonkwo took eight hundred seed-yams from Nwakibie was the worst year in living memory...That year the harvest was sad...And was also the year Okonkwo broke the peace and punished... (P.26)

The time-scheme of Arrow of God[8] seems to be more elaborately worked out in terms of years. But the phrase 'five years ago' occurs more as a refrain. The emphasis falls more on the events that distinguished that particular year than the precise date:

> On the day, five years ago, when the leaders of Umuaro decided to send an emissary to Okperi with white clay for peace or new- palm frond for war, Ezeulu spoke in vain. (P. 15)

> In the five years since the white man broke the guns of Umuaro (P.38)

> It was five years since Ezeulu promised the white man that he would send one of his sons to church. But it was only two years ago that he fulfilled the promise. (P.45)

Time seems to move in a much more leisurely way than in urban industrial societies. For nothing momentous appears to have taken place during the intervening years. The memory of hurts and enmities incurred 'five years ago' are still fresh and pressing. Despite the years being numbered, the traditional 'phenomenal calendar' seems to be operating here rather than the 'numerical calendar' of the west.[9]

Time is still reckoned in relation to specific events- the war between Umuaro and Okperi, the breaking of the guns by the white man, the hostility between Ezeulu of Umuaro and Nwaka of Umunneora. Five years here denote, as do the 'twenty years or more' on Things Fall Apart, a fairly flexible period not necessarily confined to an actual mathematical division of time. If 'twenty years or more' arc sufficient to convert a living person (0konkwo) into a legend, 'five years' indicate a span whose events still possess an immediacy with respect to the community's life.

Again, the tendency to mythicize even significant events aptly captured in the formula, 'the story was told':

> 'Abame has been wiped out,' said Ibaraki. 'it is a strength and terrible story.' (*Things Fall Apart*, p. 124)

> 'The story of what these soldiers did in Abame was still told with fear. (*Arrow of God,* p. 280)

Here Achebe is making an actual historical reference to the resistance offered by the natives of Abame to the first British pertaining to the members of the communal repertoire:

The story was told in Umuofia of how father Unoka had gone to consult the oracle of the Hills and the Caves to find out why" he always had a miserable harvest. (*Things Fall* Apart, P.15)

The story that (the white man had whipped Obika spread through the villages. (*Arrow of God,* P. 87)

The fact that the tribal, cyclic consciousness of time has been supplanted by the clock-time of the Western industry and office in the world of Obi and Odili does not prevent the primeval perception asserting itself every now and then.[10] In A Man of the People[11], Odili combines in numerical awareness of hours with a traditional leisureliness in dissecting time:

I had not always disliked Mr. Nangi. Sixteen years or so ago he had been my teacher (p.2)

The story had it that many years ago when Mr. Nwege was a poor, hungry elementary school teacher. (p.13)

The traditional manner of relating information still persists in
Odili's style,

They said this woman was a very close friend of the minister's...(P.15)

A common saying in the country after independence was that it didn't matter what you knew but who *you* know. (P.1)

It is agreed that the degree of repetition present in oral works if employed in writing would be tedious. Marjorie Winters explains that repetitiousness in written texts often leads to redundancy.[12] But redundancy, she states, goes together with clarity. Redundancy clarifies, underlines and reinforces. The garrulous narrative voice of Achebe's novels abounds in redundancies. It provides many details where one would suffice.

It repeats and recapitulates at every possible opportunity:

> The drums were still beating, persistent, and unchanging. Their sound was no longer a separate thing from the living village. It was like the pulsation of its heart. It throbbed in the air, in the sunshine, and even in the trees, and filled the village with excitement. (*Things Fall Apart,* P.40)

The opening of this passage introduces an idea which is repeated in the following two sentences. The drumbeat, indissoluble from the living village in the first, is defined as 'the pulsation of its heart' in the second. Its oneness is demonstrated by the way it permeates every 'living' aspect of the village- 'the air', 'the sunshine', even 'the trees.' Repetition serves the function of defining and explicating. It simplifies, it lessens the task of comprehension in the listener's mind.[13]

It provides several examples to reinforce an idea and attempts to explore it from every possible perspective: Perhaps in his heart Okonkwo was not a cruel man. lint his whole life was dominated by fear, the fear of failure and weakness. It was deeper and more intimate than the fear of evil and capricious gods and of magic, the fear of the forest, and of the forces of nature, malevolent, red in tooth and claw.

> Okonkwo's fear was greater than these. It was not external but lay deep within himself, lest he should be found to resemble his father. *(Things Fall Apart,* P.13)

The listing of the various fears, 'the fear of evil and capricious gods...forces of nature', accentuates the shared, communal phobias. Against these arc placed the personal, internal anxieties of Okonkwo spelt as the 'fear of failure and weakness'. Achebe emphasises Okonkwo's isolation first by defining the communal framework and then by underlining the private nature of Okonkwo's insecurity. The passage illustrates the process by which the oral artist communicates with his audience, repeating for the sake of making his meaning clear, citing repetitious analogies to drive home his point. This is a manner eminently suited to the bard and to the novelist who desires to educate the 'alien' as well as the 'alienated' in the grandeur of the African past.

The predilection for elaboration and explanation in the traditional bard is associated with his pedagogic function. The etiological ending, 'that was how', underlines the bard's responsibility to answer the unvoiced queries in his audience's mind, to transmit the wisdom of his race, to explain the reason and motives for happenings. Achebe's resorting to the etiological formula, reflected a desire to leave very few questions unanswered, to explain motives and compulsions that give rise to a certain action or behaviour:

That was how Okonkwo came to know that agbala was not only another name for a woman, it could also mean a man who had taken no title. *(Things Fall Apart,* p.13)

The man who had contradicted him had no titles. That was why he had called him a woman. (*Things Fall Apart,* 24)

He must go on treating his grown children like little boys, and if they ever said so there was a big quarrel. This was why the older his children grew the more he seemed to dislike them. (*Arrow of God,* P.91)

Repetition, in oral narrative, is justified as a mnemonic aid. But redundancy and digressiveness are also related to the general expansive tendency of the oral narrative. The same digressive pattern is typical of Achebe's novels.

Okonkwo did not have the start in life which many young men usually had. He did not inherit a barn from his father. There was no barn to inherit. The story was told in Umuofia of how his father, Unoka, had gone to consult the oracle of the Hills and the Caves to find out why he always had a miserable harvest. *Things Fall Apart,* P. 15)

A couple of pages later the narrator resumes the same theme almost with the very word with which he left off:

With a father like Unoka, Okonkwo did not have the start in life which many young men had. He neither inherited a barn nor a title, nor even a young wife.(p.17)

Isidore Okpewho explains this method as the 'ring composition'.[14] The natural accretive impulse of the barn, he asserts, leads him to inflate and expand. In the passage above, for example, while recounting the tale of Okonkwo's career, the narrator makes a long detour which focuses not on Okonkwo but on his father Unoka. So the narrative first digresses into a description of the oracle Unoka consulted and then goes on to give a detailed account of Unoka's conversation with the priestess of oracle. But despite his fondness for digressing, the 'bard' cannot afford to lose the thread of the main narrative.

Therefore, he must return from Unoka to Okonkwo again. The 'ring'- the resumption of the theme with a repetition of the previous utterance- ensures and brings about stabilisation and control.

The digressive structures flow over into the urban scene of *No Longer At Ease*[15] as well:

> Mother's room was the most distinctive of the whole house, except for father's. The difficult in deciding arose from the fact that one could not compare incomparable things. Mr. Okonkwo believed utterly and completely in the things of the white man and the symbol of (the white man's power was the written word.... Mother's room on the other hand, was full of mundane things. She had her box of clothes on a stool. On the other side of the room were pots of solid palm-oil with which she made black soap. (pp. 14-5).

The promise of a description of 'mother's room' leads to a digressive account of father's. A couple of paragraphs after the narrative returns to mother's occupations.

The 'ring composition' observed in the earlier novel is seen in this section as well.

The paratactic construction of the texts, ostensibly in conformity with the spontaneous, improvised procedure of oral composition, is designed to produce clarity. Majorie Winter, commenting on the high incidence of connectives in Achebe's *Things Fall Apart*, asserts that they account for the lucidity of his style.[16]

There is great variety in the manner in which the connective is employed:

> Unoka loved it all, and he loved the first kites that returned with the dry season, and the children who sang songs of welcome to them. (p.5)

> And what made it worse in Okonkwo's case was that he had to support his mother and two sisterrs from his meagre harvest. And supporting his mother also meant supporting his father. (p.21)

Arrow of God reveals a larger occurrence of 'but':

> But many people trembled for him that night in his compound when lie had ;ill bur threatened Ulu.... But it did not follow that Ulu would also allow himself, .. (p. 39)

More interesting, however, is the employment of the double connection 'and so', Achebe finds in this combination an ideal way of summarizing the context of an elaborate argument or for underlining the effect of a certain action:

And so Okonkwo was ruled by one passion- to hate everything that his father Unoka loved. (P. 13)

And so Nwoye was developing into a sad-faced youth. (P. 13)

The recurrence of parataxis in Achebe's works relates him to the oral story telling traditions of Nigeria which carried on method may be traced in Achebe's urban novels as well. The employment of a first-person narrator in A man of the people, who is so obviously 'telling' his story, permits the introduction of paratacdc structures.

And when I got to the ward and was told with pointless brusqueness by a girl-nurse that my patient had been discharged yesterday I felt really downcast? so I drove from the hospital to Edna's place, although her father had told me three days earlier never to set foot in his house again. And for the first time since my return from Bori my luck was on. Edna was in and her father was out. (P. 104)

But similar structures can be seen in *No Longer at Ease* as well:

After this there was another long silence. Then his father spoke, but not about the thing that was on their mind. (P. 250)

Therefore, oral linguistic style seems to be adapted in the delineation of the contemporary Nigeria milieu in the Urban novels too.

The distinction between the referential, denotative language of fiction and the poetic, figurative, oral idiom appears to have been blurred in the modern poetic novel. But Emmanuel Obiechina sees a difference between the two. He shows that the poetic language of a Western writer is merely an imposition of a 'personal pattern of linguistic expression on life through his art' where as the metaphoric style of west African novelists is the 'reproduction of a social linguistic reality'.[17]

The concrete, metaphoric idiom of oral literature is not a poeticisation of reality but a distinct mode of perception. Below are cited two descriptions of African rains, one by Karen Blixen in *Out of Africa*[18] and the other by Achebe:

> But when the earth answered like a sounding-board in deep fertile roar, and the world sang round you in all dimensions, all above and blow-that was the rain. It was like corning back to the sea, when you have been a long time away from it, like a river's embrace. *(Out of Africa,* P.41)

> And so nature was not interfered with in the middle of the rainy season. Sometime it poured down in such thick sheets of water that earth and sky seemed merged in one grey wetness. It was then uncertain whether the low rumbling of Amadiora's thunder came from above or blow.(*Things Fall Apart*, P.31)

Each passage captures the rain in dual images, visual and the other aural. Against Achebe's accurate, precise account ('it poured down in such thick sheets of water') is the highly subjective, personalized analog)? of the long awaited meeting with the lover visualized by Karen Blixen.

But Achebe extends the literal- 'poured down such thick sheets of water'- with the allusive- 'earth and sky seemed merged in one grey wetness'.

The analogy is heightened by reference to the traditional, folk theme of the relationship between sky and earth. He repeats this method while describing the sound of rain. He sees it as the 'rumbling of Amadiora's thunder' reflecting therefore the native's tendency to apotheosize elemental forces and to regard natural phenomena as manifestations of divine desires. Moreover, Achebe's is no personal metaphor but a part of the shared poetic analogy. There is also, in Achebe, a propensity towards investing natural objects with human qualities:

Yam, the king of crops, was a man's crop. (P.21)

Yam, the king of crops, was a very exacting king. (P.31)

This reverential attitude towards planting yam can never find expression in a bland statement like, 'coffee-growing is a long job'. *(Out of Africa, P.18)* The oral mind does not search for appropriate, catching embellishments. It displays a natural inclination for analogical explanation:

His power was no more than the power of a child over a goat that was said to be his. As long as the goat was alive it could be his, he would find it food and take care of it. But the day it was slaughtered he would know soon enough who the real owner was. (*Arrow of God,* P.3)

40

Perhaps Akubuebue was the only man in Umuaro who knew that tile chief priest was helpless; that a thing greater than nte had been caught in nte's trap. (*Arrow of God*, P.219)

This is pure oral poetry, the art of conversation that is regarded so highly among the Igbos. *Out of Africa,* the memoirs of Baroness Blixen, belongs to the genre of belles-lettres.

Chapter 3

Relearning the Song that Truly Speaks

I. Marques

Two stories from Mia Couto's collection *Contos do Nascer da Terra* (Stories of the Birth of the Land)1 published in 1997 "The Little Girl Without Words: Second Story For Rita" and "The Little Moon-bird: First Story For Rita," demonstrate how the Mozambican contemporary writer recreates the traditional African holistic (choric/ animistic) 'self' via the use of innovative language and narrative techniques –a self that has been overshadowed by both the colonial and postcolonial orders. Some similarities that exist between African traditional worldviews (epistemologies) and other worldviews such as Western psychoanalysis and Buddhism, could point to the idea that we might all have more in common than we think.2 We all seem to yearn for the connection with our choric/holistic self, even if often we do not know how to regain that connection due to the general fragmentation and spiritual alienation that tends to pervade our rationally ordered modern societies.

Couto's stories are generally characterized by a great emphasis on the traditional pre-colonial African ways of life and epistemologies: myth, orature, different cosmogonies, conceptions of time, the inter-relation between the world of the living and the world of the dead, as well as animistic and holistic perceptions of life, where humans, nature and the universe at large are connected in deep ways and often not perceived as separate entities. The characters of the stories are often people who live in rural areas, which in fact constitute the vast majority of Mozambique's citizens, or people who do not adhere completely to and show resistance towards the assimilation of Western cultural values brought about by both the colonization and post-colonization processes. This suggests that Couto is interested in displaying the rural side of Mozambique, the side less touched by Western cultural values, less touched by the colonization and post-colonization processes: the endogenic/internal (or choric/coric) side of Mozambican cultures. As David Rothwell notes,

> Couto has always demonstrated an awareness of Portuguese and, more generally, Western influence on his work. Rather than recusing such influence, he understands and then distorts it. He disrupts the paradigms of Western orthodoxy as he fashions identity by turning European epistemology into a raw, repackageable material. (28)

Rothwell further avers that

> Couto's propensity to dissolve boundaries is apparent, particularly those frontiers that enforce the demarcations of Western tradition. The resultant identity he writes is premised on fluidity, and challenges the rigidity of the systems, both colonial

and Marxist, imported from Europe that have dominated Mozambique for most of its history. In the latter phase of his writing, his disavowal of the postmodern project, through an attack on the International Community's invasion of Mozambican sovereignty, logically completes the postmodern and the nationalist strands in his work. He can justifiably be termed a postmodern nationalist.3 (28)

Most of the characters in Couto's writings4 seem to be living in the colonial or postcolonial present since there are many implicit or explicit references to those historical timeframes. Yet we often sense a strong resistance to those historical realities on the part of the characters. That resistance is frequently accompanied by a sense of loss, a feeling of nostalgia or a confusion (an existential nausea of sorts), which suggest that the characters live in a time of deep cultural crisis, in a society that is robbing them of what they value most and what their ancestors have believed for thousands of years. This feeling might be similar to what the anthropologist W. E. H. Stanner calls "a kind of vertigo in living" (qtd. in Chamberlin, If This Is 80) felt by the Aborigines of New Guinea, as a result of land displacement and cultural impositions brought about by the colonization process. Couto places the following message in his introduction to Stories of the Birth of the Land:

It is not the light of the sun that we lack. For millions of years the big star has been illuminating the earth and despite that we have not really learned how to see. The world needs to be seen under another light: the moonlight, that clarity that falls with respect and tenderness. Only the moonlight reveals the feminine side

44

of beings. Only the moon reveals the intimacy of our terrestrial dwelling-place. It is not the rising of the sun that we need. We lack the birth of the land. (7)

This statement is illustrative of the overall nature of the stories included in the collection and of the didactic (and thus political nature) of Couto's stories: it suggests that Mozambique needs to rebuild its identity by looking at (and rediscovering) the land and its old ways. It further suggests that Mozambican identity must come from within that land and not from the outside, or at least not merely from the outside. What Mozambique needs is not necessarily (or certainly not only) the knowledge and the development traditionally associated with the modern world and the West, which has tended to value reason, technology, objectivity, compartmentalization, intellect and masculinity over unconscious, emotion, nature, imagination, femininity and an epistemology of holism.5 Couto is asserting Mozambique's need to reawaken its non-masculine, non-rational, non-conscious, sacralized, mystical and mythical side so that the old Mozambican epistemologies can be rescued and reinvented and a truer Mozambique can then emerge –a more 'authentic' nation where all Mozambicans will be able to see, place, cherish and express themselves, and where the old epistemologies are taken into account.

"The Little Girl Without Words" is about a little girl who cannot speak, or better yet, cannot make herself understood. The girl's inability to communicate causes great pains for her father and mother as well as the rest of her community:

The little girl did not speak any words. No vowel would come out of her; her lips were occupied only with sounds that did not add up to three or four. It was a language that belonged only to her, a personal and intransmissible dialect? (87)

In an attempt to make the little girl speak, and in order to communicate and connect with her, the father tries all kinds of methods: he holds her hands tightly, speaks to her tenderly and patiently, implores her to speak, cries out of frustration, takes her to the beach, and finally decides to tell her what seems to be a very unrealistic story. In the end, the story proves to be the very medium that allows for the beginning of communication between father and daughter. This story occupies a place of great importance in Couto's collection and, perhaps, even in Couto's overall writings, including the novels, poetry and short stories. The story, which is a series of mise-en-abîmes, a story within a story, within a story, within a story... can also be seen as the mise-en-abîme par excellence (the big Russian doll, as it were), for it brings to the forefront many of the cultural identity problems affecting contemporary Mozambique, and it even offers a solution for them. One of the main characteristics of stories which employ the mise-en-abîme as a medium, is that they aim at teaching the reader something. In the case of Couto's story, the teaching is in fact multidimensional-- and the existence of the mise-en-abîme can be detected at many levels: structural, semantic, morphological and symbolical. All these levels work together to give the story an even more unified and coherent character, which in itself is yet another mise-en-abîme and serves to further reinforce Couto's cultural agenda: the illustration (display) of the metaphysical holistic conception of the world, as shared by traditional Mozambicans.

Couto's use of language and storytelling techniques shows us how language and narration assume the character of tricksters and how such a quality serves different and very important purposes; it brings wonder to storytelling, it creates suspense, and it keeps our soul alive by connecting us with that which is beyond our reach, that which is beyond language: the uncanny. But the uncanny always remains uncanny: just like Couto's language which by mixing words and inventing new terms, is constantly playing tricks and evading our understanding. Couto's language becomes similar to "dread talk" as used by the Rastafarians in Jamaica. In the same way that "dread talk" symbolized the forging of a new identity (or better, yet, an identity for the very first time) and the refusal or contesting of the colonial cultural legacy for the Caribbean people, so does Couto's language function as the agent that permits the reinvention or building of a new Mozambican identity --an agent that takes history in its own hands, so to speak, by appropriating the language of the colonizer and changing it to accommodate present cultural Mozambican needs, to affirm its own and unique way of life. Moreover, like "dread talk," Couto's language seems to be an attempt to restore the wonder of language, its power to connect us with the mystical forces, the unknown, the spiritual, giving us a strength that helps us bear the difficulties of life. As J. Edward Chamberlin puts it,

> One of the strategies of the Rastafari has been to rename things. It's an old trick, as colonizers have realized for centuries. I have seen maps of Canada where as many as a dozen different names are

layered onto one place, reflecting the different traditions of people who live (or lived) there... The Rastafarian renaming, too, has involved turning language around so that it reflects their own imaginings and recovers their realities [...]. The signature of "dreadlocks" of Rastafari are a way of catching the mysterious power, or of not losing it [...]. (Chamberlin, If This Is 187-8)6

Couto's constant use of the mise-en-abîme, in all its different manifestations, ends up creating a special effect. When reading the story/stories, one might have the impression that one is entering a circling or whirling dance, a cascade of sorts, a musical realm even, a place where we might feel detached from ourselves and experience the universe with all its powerful energy –as if we were in a state of trance or spiritual ecstasy. Thus Couto's writing teaches at least two things: that traditional (old) epistemologies have something wonderful to offer, and also that, when used well and 'strangely', language can become the very medium that allows one to experience the beauty and power of what lies beyond our grasp and to reach spiritual fulfillment.

"The Little Girl Without Words" has a subtitle: "Second Story for Rita". Such title occupies a central importance in the story, for it suggests that the 'true' meaning of the story is not what it might at first appear to be. Put differently, the 'true' meaning is not, or at least not only, the first meaning, but rather the second meaning, or even the third or the fourth meaning. The true meaning is to be found in the metaphoric, the poetic, the unobvious, the hidden, or in the untold/unwritten even. Not only does the second (sub) title tell us literally that the story has a "second" story imbedded in itself, but it also appears within brackets, as if reinforcing once again (visually in the text) the idea of the importance of going behind what we see and literally read throughout the story: the idea of looking beyond the material/real possibility, and ultimately, beyond language and its meaning. Thus, the subtitle of the story is the very first mise-en-abîme of the many others that are displayed throughout the rest of story: it is the first Russian doll, enveloping the many other little ones that are to come out after our careful reading of the Great Mother. This Great Mother functions as the protective womb enveloping all the children inside her: like a goddess who wants us to know/feel the immensity of what exists, and at the same time, does not fully (or rationally) show us that very immensity because that very knowing/showing would kill the transcendental aspect of the divine, which is untranslatable and unnamable.

But surprises (tricks) never end and so… a more careful (deeper) reading of the (first) title will tell us that in reality it already contains the "second story" of the story, for the title does not say that the little girl is mute, but rather that she possesses no words –which is not the same thing. In fact, being able to speak without words might be a better way of speaking, if we take into account the idea that words are only an arbitrary (and thus incomplete) system, invented by humans to name and comprehend that which is ultimately un-nameable and incomprehensible to us in its true dimension. This reading of the first title makes sense, for in the story we do discover that the little girl speaks through music-like sounds and thus, possesses a language. In that case then, the first title is already a big Russian doll (or the Great Mother) with many little dolls (or children) inside, ready to be played with and also play "the player".

Couto has stated the following:

> The secret, in my case, is to transport the childhood.
> [...]. We all have preserved in ourselves that
> childhood, which people have taught us how to tame,
> how to forget, how to look at as an unproductive
> place. Children do not fit well into our present
> concept of what it means to be productive,
> responsible. [Yet] that childhood has survived in all
> of us. (My translation, in Jeremias 2)

As the opening paragraph of "The Little Girl Without
Words" indicates, the little girl does indeed possess a
language, but one that no one understands. Why does no
one understand it? Little girls (and little boys) often have a
language of their own, one that is highly poetic, musical,
fluid and which does not obey the rules of adult language.
In a fashion similar to Julia Kristeva and others, Couto
seems to believe that children speak a pre-symbolic
language, a language which is detached from social
connotations and where gender roles and other assigned
social roles and classifications of the world, things and
people in general, do not yet exist or are not yet formed.
Children are close to what Kristeva[7], following Plato (67)
calls the chora, that sacred or sacralized (and whole, in the
sense of being un-fragmented, un-dichotomized) side which
allows them to listen to all their unconscious/subjective
intelligence –imagination, instinct, emotion, body, and so
on. That chora is broken (or at least suppressed and
disrupted) when children enter the symbolic world of the
adults which imposes roles, regulations and classification
on the world and people based on the so-called higher
intelligence –reason, science, objectivity, culture, and so

forth. This is why the adults do not quite understand children and the world they live in, and also the reason why one can suggest that the father of this little girl does not understand her. In this story, the father has entered the rational adult world and thus broken (or suppressed) his contact with the world of the little girl (the world of his 'little boy,' so to speak)--a world which obeys different linguistic and cognitive patterns. But his chora still exists inside of him: it is preserved/kept somewhere, as Couto suggests above, and it only needs to be brought to the surface. In psychoanalytical terms, this loosely means that the chora of the 'little boy'/father has been pushed to the very back of his unconscious; it has been repressed because adult life and society do not value/favour it, and consider it immature and inferior to the so-called higher intelligences associated with adult life.

The father loves his little girl (and his 'little boy') dearly and so he wants to 'find' them, to understand them, to reconnect with them. He suffers immensely from the fact that he cannot speak to and reach them. The father knows (senses, feels) that the language spoken by them is beautiful: "so beautiful as to enchant," so beautiful as to "imprison [him] in the intonation," and so "touching" (87) that it has the power to make one cry. It is a language that sounds more like a song, a song of yearning for something beautiful and powerful and good--something that one has lost and wants back madly –but does not really know how to bring/call back to us. The song-language sung by the little girl, awakens in the father a powerful urge, an almost visceral need; it is like a demand, seemingly as strong as the one expressed in Derek Walcott's poem "Sainte Lucie": "come back to me, my language, come back cacao, grigri, solitaire, ciseau the scissor-bird" (309). "Fala comigo filha!" (87) ('Speak to me daughter!'), says the father to the girl. It is the magnitude of the father's urge that makes him search for ways to communicate with his daughter (just like Walcott makes use of all kinds of words [i.e., French, English, Spanish, Creole] in an attempt to create a language that will 'tell him' as accurately as any language can allow):

> Her father would dedicate a lot of attention and affliction to her. One night he held her hands tightly and implored, certain that he was speaking to himself:
> - Speak to me daughter!
> His eyes gave in. The little girl kissed the tear. She tasted that salty water and said:
> - Sea...
> The father was surprised from mouth to hear. Had she spoken? He jumped and shook his daughter's elbows. See, you can speak, she speaks, she speaks! He would scream so that people could hear him. She said sea, she said sea, the father would repeat throughout the house. The relatives came running and leaned over her. But no other intelligible sound was announced... (87-8)

The communication between father and daughter is hard to achieve. Yet, the need for that communication to happen is so great that it forces the father to keep searching deeper and deeper inside himself, to see if he can find the magic word that will 'speak' to his daughter. Finally, he does come to a brilliant idea: to tell his daughter a story. This idea works. The idea of the story comes to the father because it had in fact never left him; it was in some part of his unconscious self and just needed to be called back to 'conscious' life: it was there, underneath, like a latent, soft lullaby8, just waiting and wanting to be brought to the surface, so that the father could feel the wonder again --the wonder of feeling whole, connected, unbroken, the wonder of entering the choric realm:

> It was then that it came to him: his daughter could only be saved by a story! And right there he invented one [...]. When he arrived at that point the father lost voice and became quiet. The story had lost its string and thread inside his head. Or perhaps it was the cold from the water which was already covering his feet, and the legs of his daughter? And in a desperate state, he said: - Now, it will never be. Right away, the little girl got up and walked through the waves. The father followed her, scared. He saw his daughter pointing at the sea. [...] -Daughter please, come back. Slow down, daughter, please... Rather than stepping back, the little girl penetrated further into the sea. Then, she stopped and passed her hand through the water. The liquid scar closed itself, instantaneously. And the sea restored itself, it became one. The little girl walked back, took her father's hand and guided him back home. Above, the moon recomposed itself. - See father? I finished your story. And both of them, illuminated, vanished from the room, which they had never left. (88-9)

The story told to the little girl is a story where doubt is suspended: it is a story that makes (and gives sense) to the world, without concerning itself with truth boundaries. It is a story (seemingly) very unrealistic which merges the real and the imaginary, reason and unreason, possible and impossible; it is a story full of trickery, as if we were in fact dealing with a real trickster who is constantly tricking us into believing things that are unreal or seemingly opposite.9 The bridge between such opposites can, of course, be questioned, if we argue that the stories or histories or theories that explain the world and ourselves to ourselves are in fact all human makings –made out of an arbitrary language system– and so we end up with all kinds of 'fabulous' stories about who we are, what we must do, feel, eat, dress and how it is that the world or universe 'really' functions. As well argued by Edward Chamberlin in If This Is Your Land, Were Are Your Stories?Finding Common Ground, many (if not all) of the stories (and thus histories) informing and giving sense to our lives, are make-up/made-up fables, which serve to ease our existential nausea, hide our ignorance, fragility and fears of the unknown –and yet, also fables that make us feel at home and give sense and purpose to our lives.

Couto's first lesson then seems to be that we must all try to reconnect with the world of our childhood, the world of wonder, the world of the chora –it is a lesson for all the adults of the world. But the story aims at much more than that. The story can (and should) be read directly in the socio-cultural context of Mozambique. The use of the little girl and father metaphor in this story can be taken as another trick used by Couto to point to the multiple meanings of his stories.

Before further exploring the relationship of this story with the Mozambican socio-cultural environment, a look at the other story included in the collection, "The Little Moonbird: First Story for Rita," is necessary. This story precedes "The Little Girl Without Words." This means of course that "The Little Girl without Words" can be taken as a continuation of the first story --a reasoning reinforced by the fact that it has the subtitle of "Second Story for Rita." This does not invalidate the previous argument pertaining to the subtitle of the second story and its function as the first mise-en-abîme of the second story. It actually reinforces it by suggesting that each single story in Couto's collection always contains multiple messages or stories in it, and that what each story says is always incomplete: its meaning always surpasses what it openly says, what the eye can directly catch. Moreover, the first story ends with the question "And then what happens father?" --indicating that the story has not been completed, at least not according to the little girl who was receiving it from the father. In fact, in the first story the father is frustrated with the little girl, for every night she demands a story from him and when he tells her one, she never seems satisfied with its ending and always asks the same (stubborn) question: "And then father what happens?" At the structural level, the first story also contains two stories: the one about the girl and the one about the bird.

After telling the little girl several stories, and not being able to satisfy her constant thirst for knowledge or wonder, the father decides to tell her the story of a bird whose dream was to fly to the moon:

> My daughter has a painful time falling asleep. No one knows the fears that sleep brings to her. Every night I am called to my duty as a father and I invent her a lullaby. I always perform that duty poorly. When I am trying to end the story she asks me for more: - And then what happens? What Rita wants is for the entire world to fall asleep. And she always argues a dream that might

happen in her sleep: she wants to become the moon. The little girl wants to travel to the moon, and, she tells the two of us, so that I become the land, and she the moon. The Mozambican traditions are still inflating her lunar courtship. [...]. Once upon a time a little bird was dreaming in its little roost. It would look at the moonlight and it would make fantasies go up in the sky. Its dream would become more immense: - I will land there, in the moon... (67)

The story about the bird is of course also a story about the little girl and her constant craving for stories of wonder: like the bird, the little girl seems to have dreams, needs and wishes that are far too big for her human capacity. The father's story seems to suggest that only people (and to a certain extent animals) have life: the other bodies, such as the moon are petrified, lifeless entities. It is the "moony" ('enluarado') (67) character of the bird (and little girl) that makes it lose its quality as a bird and become petrified and lifeless. The adjective "enluarado," used to describe the bird here has a second meaning; it is yet another Russian doll, for it implies that the bird suffered from mad ideas, reason why it wanted to fly to the moon.10

Thus, the first story has many messages (mise-en-abîmes). At first glance, it would seem to re-enforce the idea that when one has a dream, a need or a wish, one should try to fulfill it, and if one can not realistically fulfill it, one must resort to the power of the imagination in order to get it, for the imagination can have the power to fulfill our most grand desires. If it happens in the realm of the imagination, it becomes as real and fulfilling as if it were to happen in actual reality. As the Caribbean poet Derek

Walcott would say: "I [have] no nation now but the imagination" (350). However, a more careful reading of Couto's story will tell us that too much dreaming and unreasonable desires will lead us to madness and the loss of humanness. An analysis of the morphology of the first title of the story, will also show us that the story has at least two meanings (two more little Russian dolls ready to play), again reinforcing the idea that stories and words possess secondary hidden meanings--meanings which we must aim at understanding so that we can have access to the wonder of the infinite, the mystical, the wonder of "overstanding," as the Rastafarians might put it. First, "The little moon-bird" ('A luavezinha') can be read as "moon-neighbour" ('luavizinha'), a reading that will point to the cosmic holistic conception of the universe shared by many Mozambican groups: it implies that all the planets are deeply connected and close to each other, that the earth is in fact near the moon, like a sister of sorts. By extension, this also implies that birds and humans are part of the greater order and that is why they feel the urge to go beyond their human and animal limits and connect with the rest of the universe. On the other hand, given the closeness between the words "luavezinha" ('little moon-bird') and "levezinha" ('very light'), we can suggest that the story wants to point to the fact that the human mind (our spirit and imagination) is very light --so light in fact, that it can fly away, travel and enter other world orders, other realities, and thus experience the wonder of what lies beyond our physical reach. The story did not satisfy the little girl precisely because the imagination of the father was not light (flexible) enough to travel beyond the moon and liberate the bird, not light enough to be able to allow the bird to be both bird and moon, that is.

It is precisely because of the 'heaviness' of the father's imagination that the little girl remains unsatisfied with the story and demands more with the question "and then father?" Ultimately, the little girl is the metaphor for the Mozambican land, its people and their holistic or sacralized conception of the universe. The little girl is the nation of Mozambique and the father represents the governing elite of colonial and post-colonial states. The constantly repeated question of the little girl "and then father?" has multiple meanings and functions. On one hand, it alludes to the dissatisfaction (and loss of wonder) experienced by Mozambicans who have had their culture and way of thinking dismissed and shattered by the new, modern, secularized and compartmentalized Western order. One the other hand, and because of its constant use, this question actually re-establishes that same Mozambican world order: the repetition causes us to feel that whirling effect that I mentioned previously--the effect of something that has no end, like a cascade where all parts are interrelated and work to produce a holistic and sacralized conception of life and the universe. Again, Couto is killing at least two birds with one stone (or two rabbits with a single stroke, as we say in Portuguese).

But the father feels the dissatisfaction of the little girl. It is precisely because of the dissatisfaction of both father and daughter that the father comes back with another story, a second story, which as it turns out, proves to be much more effective. The little girl's muteness is related to the fact that the new order governing the country does not value or really understand the old Mozambican epistemologies. In other words, it is not purely a matter of the semantics of the language –that is, the fact that the majority of Mozambicans speak Bantu languages and the small elite running the country speak Portuguese, which is the official language of Mozambique– although that of course plays an intrinsically role.11 In the story, Couto actually resolves the issue of separation between the world of the father and that of the little girl, the world of the Mozambican colonial and/or post-colonial state and its citizens and thus the culturally and linguistically alienated situation of most Mozambicans. The Kristevan choric self now becomes symbol of the Mozambican land: its people and its traditions, a self that must be reawakened to feed/teach the new order –a choric self that had been relegated to the periphery of the state's interests in the name of modernization and civilization. The choric self then, becomes the universe at large, where all the elements are joined and where the human self becomes de-centered, only to experience what can be termed as the force of the universe, or God.

This choric self is what in astronomy would correspond to the time before the big-bang and what is Buddhist Zen terms would equate to the "all in one" or the "Great I"12, which is also the state that allows for nirvana (emptiness of thought) to occur, a state that 'resides' beyond language and thus is indescribable through it--a state of bliss and mystical apprehension. In its original platonic sense, the chora refers to that place that merges all the elements: air, water, earth, fire, a place of high power and energy that will give origin to everything –this is why Plato calls it the "nurse of all becoming and change" (67). In Christian terms, these would loosely equate to the "De Profundis" of Psalm 129. All these senses of the choric self are similar to each other, which only serves to show that different traditions (Western and otherwise) do in fact share many of the same underlying beliefs.

Thus, from the child's choric self, Couto moves us to the adult (repressed) choric self, to the Mozambican (repressed) choric self, and then he shows us (discloses) all the choras and the wonder that lies there awaiting to be embraced: he is the teacher, teaching us how to dance in the whirls of the greater or larger life. The language sung by the little girl made people cry because it reminded them of the Mozambican choric self, the self that they had forgotten how to connect with and buried deep inside them. Their cry symbolizes their loss and profound yearning and desire to reconnect with the grand order of the universe their ancestors once had. That is why the father goes to great extents to (re)learn the language of the little girl.

It is important to note that it is the emotion (and not the 'reason') of the father that first speaks to the little girl. He had tried all kinds of words and ways to achieve communication with his daughter and yet she had remained mute (and deaf). When the father cries out of desperation, she mumbles what seems to be her very first intelligible word: "sea". On a larger symbolical level, the tear shed by the father has many other meanings. Being a fluid substance, the tear can symbolize the letting go of the individual self and the entering in the choric/cosmic self. This is further supported by the fact that it is by the sea that the girl will finally find a way to speak and be understood by the father. The house (the father) represents the individualized human self, which tends to dichotomize and separate things, whereas the sea represents the decentered or choric self. The sea is the place that can 'liquidize' both the father and the girl so that they can finally enter the larger cosmic realm.13 It is in the sea that we witness the disintegration of the entire world. It is in the sea that all becomes shattered and the order of the universe is lost but also re-established: it is there that we witness the 'all becoming one', or the 'one becoming all' and thus the holistic African conception of the universe is restored. The moon breaks down, the sea opens up and the earth bleeds. Blood becomes indistinguishable from water and the water indistinguishable from blood. Sand becomes silver and silver becomes sand. It is the end of the world. Or so the father thought. But then the little girl takes charge of the story and literally jumps inside it to help the father reconstruct the cosmic order, to literally give birth to the land.

As in the first story, the father's imagination has not been flexible enough to continue the story he is telling. His rational and compartmentalized self, not used to intricate exercises of the mind, becomes numb: it loses the story's "string" and "thread" (89). He is flexible enough to disrupt the order of the world, but not ingenious enough to re-establish it again. He becomes afraid of the unknown, of that which cannot be measured in rational terms: he becomes afraid of his unconscious, of the dark places of the world, of the universe at large which he cannot measure in human (and Western) quantities, for it escapes his smallness. The little girl is the one who saves both of them and the world from finally disappearing:

> Right away, the little girl got up and walked through the waves. The father followed her, scared. He saw his daughter pointing the sea. Then he could see a glimpse of it: in the entire extension of the ocean, a deep crack. The father was surprised with that unexpected fracture, fantastic mirror of the story he had just invented. A deep strange fear invaded his entrails. Would it be in that abyss that they would

both disappear? - Daughter please, come back. Delay yourself, daughter, please... (89)

At the structural level, this story (like the first one) contains more than one story. It has at least three: the one being told to Rita about the little girl who did not speak, the one about Rita (or is it the little girl of the story being told?) literally taking over and finishing the father's story, and the one told in the last line, indicating that father and daughter had never left the room, even though we might have thought they did. Thus, this story (like the first one) further reinforces the idea that imagination is indeed very powerful, and that words give meaning and sense to that which is meaningless and disorganized: words weave the world, literally reinventing it for us, giving sense to the senseless, and ultimately having the power to make us feel safe at home. This serves to show the central importance of orally transmitted knowledge in traditional African cultures; it shows that the mere act of telling a story makes the events being told real; in other words, it demonstrates the magical power of storytelling and language. This magical power can also apply to written stories since language in general (written or oral) is capable of creating an entire world system, of giving meaning to that which has no a priori meaning. As Hampâté Bâ puts it,

> One peculiarity of the African memory is its restoring the recorded event in its entirety, like a film that unreels from beginning to end, and restoring it in the present. It is a matter not of remembering, but of bringing up into the present a past event in which everyone participates --the person who is reciting and his audience. The whole art of the storyteller lies in

that. No one is a storyteller unless he can report a thing as it happened 'live' in such a way that his hearers, like himself, become new living, active witnesses of it. (qtd. in Unesco: A General History of Africa 109)

It is precisely this "entirety," the restoring of the past event "in the present" and the "bringing up into the present a past event" pointed out by Bâ that Couto's story tries to reconstruct in the story of the little girl, thus showing his engagement in recreating the reality of African oral traditions. In this story the father does indeed re-learn the old ways; he gets in touch with his little girl, and consequently, with his nation. Let us hope that, like the father, the post-colonial state will also be open enough to allow non-Western epistemologies to be nurtured in Mozambique so that all can sing the song that truly speaks, the song of the little girl, who in reality might be the most mature of all. And she sings beautifully indeed.

Chapter 4

Comparing the Child Hero

L. N. Nwokora

IN his work on Chinua Achebe's novels, entitled 'Chinua Achebe and the Tragedy of History[1],' Thomas Melone says that the content of literature ought to be judged as "a portion of his destiny" (1973, 12). Explaining his reasons, the Cameroonian critic says that every authentic literature should be a "carrier of humanity" ("porteuse d'humanite"), since it should, whether it be African or European, "witness for man and his destiny"; because, continues the critic, "men are first of all men, their identity is fundamental, and their destiny human" (12).

More than any other form of literary criticism or appreciation, comparative literature highlights this universality of even' creative literary art. Universality, however, does not mean that one must necessarily compare authors from different countries or different cultural backgrounds. It is possible to compare and contrast two or more writers from the same country, from the same village, even from the same family, and finally, an author can be compared to himself. One comes up with interesting findings, in comparing, for example, the Chinua Achebe of *No Longer at Ease* with the Achebe of *Arrow of*

God. The young graduate returning from England, unable to find his feet in his former home, and the village of Umuaro no longer the same under sweeping religious attacks on the gods that had hitherto guaranteed its security and unity, both are witnesses each in its own way to the same cracking society under the invasion of foreign culture. Does it mean that the celebrated Nigerian novelist has said everything when he published his famous *Things Fall Apart*, and that thereafter is he only repeating himself Far from it?

The novelist is comparable to a surveyor, whose field is the human society; in each novel he observes society from a particular point of view. The product of his artistic (here literary) creation is a "portion" of man's struggle with life, i.e., with his destiny, and this "odyssey" reproduces, *mutatis mutandis*, similar characteristics, whether it talks of Achilles, of Antigone, of Hamlet, of Obi Okonkwo or Ezeulu.

The above considerations help us to better appreciate Ime Ikiddeh's definition of a novel as "fiction based on an historical event recreated in human terms" (Ngugi xii). The particular point of focus of the two authors we are studying is the child in his relation to given certain "historical events recreated in human terms" in two different countries and at nearly ten years' interval in time. Before comparing these historical events viewed as recreated fiction, we should first of all ascertain why the two authors chose each a child to be his hero.

Why the Child as hero?

Poetry is best appreciated, not by reasoning, but by feeling, i.e. by entering into the ecstatic sentiments of the poet at his moment of writing. The poetic verse aims, therefore, at arousing these sentiments in the reader, and not at a logical understanding of the passage. Whereas prose may receive one clear interpretation or explanation, no one interpretation can ever exhaust the wealth of meaning couched in a few poetic verses. If it is true that a piece of literary work escapes its author once it is set down on paper, it is even truer of poetry than of any other form of creative writing. There are certain experiences in life which, in order to retain one's mental health, were better felt than reasoned about. By his age, nature, and psychological make-up, the child feels things and does not reason about them, at least in the cut and dry syllogism of the adult. The child's innocence, his openness to every instinct and desire his connivance with nature, his instinctive intransigence for purity and truth... are among the qualities that make Melone believes that the only poetic state is childhood; in the sense where the poetic state or condition may be interpreted to mean the ideal state of paradise lost. The first aim, therefore, of a novelist whose hero is a child could be the desire, conscious or not, to travel back along the slippery steps to his lost Garden of Eden.

The second reason -and this is nearer to two authors we arc studying- is that the unreasoning attitude of the child, with whom the author often identifies himself, helps to rub off the sharp edge of the cruel experiences narrated in the book. The child is by temperament elastic, his own idealism is not the dangerously stiff rigidity of an Okonkwo who commits suicide in order not to witness what Melone calls 'the glorious funerals of a dying Africa' (Melone 77). Oyono's 'house boy', ' Toundi, suffers series of humiliations, but does not commit suicide (he is actually killed by the whites while attempting to run for his life), and Ngugi's Njoroge is recalled from his suicide attempt by the voice of his mother. Okonkwo's adult pride stung him beyond recall; he had to die.

The third and final advantage of the child-hero is that, thanks to his naivety and undiluted reproduction of events, what he narrates is nobody's exclusive property. The author can therefore use him (and how apt at the hands of Oyono and Ngugi!) and hide perfectly behind his translucid frankness to relate whatever happens. Who can accuse the child of fomenting trouble, or of inciting one particular political party or ethnic group against another? Does he even feel the pinch and sting of discrimination and racism as adults do? At best he feels shocked, and registers his shock like the faithful photographic paper that he is. The most salutary aspect of the child's character is that he is completely absorbed by the present, does not ruminate on the past as adults do, and has a carefree attitude about the future (*i.e.* when this even dawns on his consciousness).

It *is* true that the heroes of *Houseboy* and *Weep Not, Child* oscillate between infancy and adolescence, but their age and experiences in the two novels are still completely characterized, on their part, by innocence and naivety of childhood.

Comparing Toundi and Njoroge

Some of the points raised here above, about the artistic benefits of the child-hero, do not apply to the two novels under consideration. While one could describe Camara Laye's *African Child* as an unbroken chaplet of one nostalgic childhood memory after another, it would be almost impossible to imagine any atom of nostalgia in Oyono's mind, or Ngugi's either, when they bend over the creation of their Toundi and Njoroge respectively. For while *The African Child* affords the Guinean undergraduate in Paris a salutary fight into fancy from the cold, indifferent, lonely and capitalist atmosphere of the French capital - exactly as Louis Guilloux's 'Pain des Reves'[12] does for the novelist from Brittany in Nazi-occupied France of 1942- the two novels being studied evoke rather the same bitter taste in the reader's mouth as Mongo Beti's *Remember Ruben.*

If nostalgia there was, it is rather for a childhood that never existed, or rather that is not allowed to exist as it should. Toundi and Njoroge belong to the generation of African children who never had any childhood - a model of which one reads in the Edenic memories recounted by the hero of *The African Child*; they rather resemble the generation of those European children born in the late thirties, and whose childhood was spent in concentration camps or in cities terrorised consistently by Nazi brutality.

A Sigmund Freud would have summed up all we have said here above in one short phrase: that sort of childhood is just a *"reve manque"*- a lost dream - if not a nightmare, like that of Morzamba in *Remember Ruben*. And who likes to recall a nightmare? Except, of course, for some very serious reasons best known to the author.

These reasons already form the subject-matter of several commentaries on Oyono and Ngugi, and will only be very briefly dealt with here. We shall now examine and compare the nightmarish experiences of the two child heroes.

Resemblances

For purpose of clarity, we would like to start this comparative study by examining the areas of resemblance or similarity between Toundi's fate and that of Njoroge.

The two heroes are both children, not just from the titles of the novels, but from indications about their age. Toundi, the personage-cum-narrator of *Houseboy* speaks about his age at the very beginning of his "dairy," explaining what - according to his own understanding - was his true reason for leaving his parental home.

> In fact I just wanted to get close to the white *man* with hair like the beard on a maize cub who dressed in women's clothes and give little black boys' sugar lumps. I was in a gang of heathen boys who followed the missionary about as he went from hut to hut... (Oyono 9)

As for Njoroge, his age is indicated right from the opening of the very first chapter of the book where his mother, Nyokabi, asks him "would you like to go to school?" (Ngugi 3). Most Africans know the relative age of any child about to start school - exceptions being made for adult education. Later on, in flashback chronology, the author, explaining how Ngotho (Njoroge's father) had become a "Muhoi", says among other things:

> Njoroge had never come to understand how his father had become a 'Muhoi.' Maybe a child did not know such matters. They were too deep for him (Ngugi 13).

The two child-heroes grew in a precarious atmosphere of colonial oppression and exploitation. Need it be stressed that this point is at the very core of the two novels under study?

Houseboy is set in the French Cameroons of between 1921-1939, i.e. between the placement of the former German protectorate (1884-1914) under French mandate, after the Allies had occupied it from 1914-1916. We have indications of this, first from the only direct allusion to "the War" in the novel from Mekongo, "the army veteran" (see Oyono 57), and then indirectly from the cook shocked by the boldness and unhealthy inquisitiveness of "youngsters of today" who pry into the secrets of the white man. Says the cook to Toundi: 'I don't understand you, you youngsters of today. In the time of the Germans we took no interest in the affairs of the whites.'(Oyono 61).

Ngugi's *Weep not, child* is set in a Kenya where the indigenes return from the white man's wars of 1914-1916, and 1939-45 to find their land gone: the white settlers now own all their land.The unsuccessful attempts to recover the lost land lead eventually to the terrorist underground movement called the "Mau-Mau". We are therefore in the Kenya of the fifties, of the liberation struggles by Jomo Kenyatta, in a Kenya as mercilessly exploited as the French Cameroon of Oyono's *Houseboy*. As a fitting explanation for the predatory appetite of the white settlers of this period, Ngugi explains, in a flashback, the genesis of the passionate love of Mr Howlands for the land (in Kenya) his almost sensual attachment to this "shamba" (Ngugi 29). And the reason is that,

> He (Mr. Howlands) was a product of the First World War. After years of security at home, he had been suddenly called to arms and he had gone to the war. With the fire of youth he imagines war a glory. Bur after four years of blood and terrible destruction, like many other young men he was utterly disillusioned by

the 'peace.' He had to escape. East Africa was a good place. *Here was a big trace of wild country to conquer* (Ngugi 30) -our own stress.

The theme of economic exploitation in the colonies has been the most common among African writers, especially in this pre- independence era. And Mr. Howlands is presented to us as one among many who, "disillusioned by the 'peace'... had to escape". They were no longer coming as mere colonialists just to keep order and levy taxes for the Imperial Crown, they had emigrated in search of a new permanent home. And what better place than this unprotected "wild country," which was a prey "to conquer"? One is not surprised therefore to hear Mr. Howlands declare peremptorily to the despoiled Ngotho (father of the child-hero): "my home is here"(32).

Ngotho tries gradually, and on several occasions to explain to little Njoroge how the land that was formerly their family property had passed into the hands of Mr. Howlands, and how he Ngotho had become a "Muhoi" (a sort of a vassal in feudal times) on his own land (Ngugi 26). But the best summary of the sad story of expropriation is given by Kiarie, one of the speakers at the rally in support of the strike embarked upon by the despoiled Kenyans:

> All the land belonged to the people –black people.
> They had been given it by God. For even- race had
> their country ... Later, our fathers were taken captives
> in the first Big war to help in a war whose course they
> never knew. And when they came back? 'Their land
> had been taken away for a settlement of the white
> soldiers... . Our people were taken and forced to work
> for these settlers.... When people rose to demand their

rights they were shot down... When the second Big War came, we were taken to fight Hitler -Hitler who had not wronged us. We were killed, we shed blood to save the British Empire from defeat and collapse. (57-58).

But now that "there was a man sent by God whose name was Jomo" (note the biblical language verbatim with the fourth Gospel), they "have gathered ... to tell the British... "The time has come. Let my people go... We want back our land! Now!" (58).

Did they get it? The "Mau Mau" was the answer.

In Oyono's *Houseboy* the tragic experience of exploited Africans is, like everything else in this fundamentally satirical novel, presented in a rather ludicrous fashion. Since the "narrator" is Toundi himself, we arc hemmed in with him in his little world of a child: we only sec what he sees, and experience what he experiences. But childish and of little consequence as Toundi's experiences may be seen, they are nevertheless pointers to a similar spirit of merciless exploitation.

The first instance of this which we meet in the novel is Toundi's joy at finding himself the boy of a white man (a rare privilege at the time!), and what is more one whom the white man has taught how to read and write. What did it matter to the child so raised in his expectations if he was paid no wages?

I am his boy, a boy who can read and write, serve Mass, lay a table, sweep out his room and make his bed. I don't earn any money. Now and then he gives me an old shirt or an old pair of trousers (Oyono15)

Exploitation of child labour? And by a missionary? Father Gilbert is only being true to a generally prevalent mentality towards Africans at the period. The second is the symbolic episode of the nightly raids on indigenes' quarters by the chief of police, nicknamed the "Gullet" ("Gosier D' Oiseau" in the original French text) because of "his long flexible neck like a tickbird's neck" (24). Toundi narrates one such visit to the house of his brother-in-law with whom he lived.

> The door gave way before I could open it. Into the tiny house charged four Ful'be constables followed by Gullet. I slipped behind the door while my brother-in-law and sister, half dead with fear, watched Gullet ... and his men overturning the bits of furniture .... Gullet kicked a water jug that shattered into pieces. He told one of his men to turn over a pile of banana bunches. He pulled off a banana and gobbled it down.... . he picked another banana and began to eat it. My sister's eyes grew round. I began to be afraid again. Gullet turned, bent his long neck and went out. The noise of the engines died away and then there was silence (24-25)

The above clearly depicts the condition of the African terrorised by armed white settlers who destroy or appropriate his belongings.

Our third and last example comes to show what easily becomes of the salary of paid African workers who have the misfortune to damage anything while on duty. Mrs. Decazy, the wife of the commandant, like any other unfaithful wife (or husband) is ever jittery and her domestics naturally bear the brunt of her cantankerous mood. If they broke any plate or dish their salary would go in compensation out of all proportion. In one of these moods, "she carried out in inspection and found a broken decanter. She fixed a price and deducted it forms the cook's wages and mine. It came to half our month's earnings" (74).

Toundi is lucky this time to paid any wage at all, and he and all the other domestics are warned that "that's only a beginning... only a beginning"(74). It is the litany of similar humiliations, which, *mutatis mutandis*, provoke the ill-fated strike in *Weep not, child.* Jacobo's ignoble role in the latter novel is comparable, in its meanness, greed and treachery to a similar role by Toundi's repugnant uncle in *Houseboy.* Unable to resist his greed for the delicious porcupine prepared by Toundi's mother, the greedy uncle advises his brother (the hero's father) against Toundi's childish misdemeanour, saying, "if you want to make him obedient... take away his food.... This porcupine is really delicious" (12).

Hence the hero, reduced to "peering through the cracks in the mud wall" of his parental hut at his father and uncle gulping down greedily his own share of the evening meal (12), is a symbol of Africans despoiled of their lawful rights through the instrumentality of those fellow Africans who arc supposed to protect and defend them. They are just like the Kenyans of *Weep not, child,* who through the treacherous puppetry of chief Jacobo (himself an indigene), become 'Muhoi' on their very ancestral lands.

The last important point of resemblance in the two novels is the use of child innocence and naivety to puncture the myth of white racial superiority. Oyono's naive Toundi leaves no aspect untouched, his symbolic "broom" sweeping through not only the official residence of the commandant and discovering Madam Decazy's contraceptives... but also through the church and the prisons where hypocrisy equally held sway. Beneath the facade of a mythical racial superiority, Toundi finds the same lying, cowardly and unimaginative brutes as one could find anywhere. Madam Decazy is the highest lady of the land being the wife of the highest white official. Was her nymphomania not exactly the same as that of the professional Africa prostitute, Kalisa? The latter had at least the honesty to accept her place and keep it. Such a sacrilegious scrutiny could not go unpunished, and Toundi paid for it with his life.

In *Weep not, child,* Njoroge and Stephen Howlands meet at an inter-schools' sports to discover to their mutual surprise that they had each secretly wanted to befriend the other, but had been held back by this mysterious "electric tension in the air..." which is nothing but racial prejudice and induced xenophobia:

> 'I used to hide near the road. I wanted to speak with some of you.'
> Stephen was losing his shyness. Why didn't you?'
> 'I was afraid.'
> …
> 'I am sorry I ran away from you. I too was afraid.'
> 'Afraid?' It was Stephen's turn to wonder.
> 'Yes. I too was afraid of you.'
> 'Strange'
> 'Yes. It's strange how you do fear something because your heart is already prepared to fear because may be *you* were brought up to fear something, or simply because you found others fearing..." (Ngugi 110)

And thanks to their world of children, which "stood somewhere outside petty prejudice, hatred and class differences," "they felt close together, united by a common experience of insecurity and fear. no one could escape" (88, 111). "No one" neither black nor white. This momentary freedom from the inhibitions of social and racial prejudices helps these two children (one white the other black) experience what is inescapably fundamental to even- human being in circumstances such as the Kenya of 'Mau Mau' terrorism, 'a common experience of insecurity and fear no one could escape.' Imprisoned hitherto in his ghetto-mentality, the black would have thought that the "superior" race should also be "superior" to feelings of fear and insecurity. After this discovery, they are never the same again, just like Toundi who, having discovered to his utter amazement that "a great chief like the Commandant (is) uncircumcised ... was relieved by this discover)'," because "it killed something inside (him)": fear. "I knew I should never be frightened of the Commandant again" (Oyono 28)

Differences

From the above points which still do not exhaust all the aspects of resemblance, it is clear that there is much in common between *Houseboy* and *Weep not child*. Let us examine the divergences in the experiences of the two child-heroes, because no matter how much destinies resemble, each is still unique in its own way. The fact that *Houseboy* is an English translation from the original French text, *Une vie de boy*, hardly merits any mention, except to stress the different colonial backgrounds in which the two novels are written. If, according to an American proverb, "the first hour is the rudder of the day," we can hardly find a better way to start a study of the divergences in these two destinies than to go back to their origin, i.e. to their family background.

While Toundi evolves as an orphan, Njoroge, is all along surrounded and protected by the warmth of his parental home. It is quite true that at the opening pages of *Houseboy* we find Toundi surrounded, like Njoroge, by the warmth of a family. But, like the "predestined personage" of Marthe Robert's "Family Novel," Toundi is not destined to "spend his childhood days with his parents, in the warmth of their common love" (Robert 52). Because his father did not love (him) as a father ought to love his son, he had his mother's "blessing" for fleeing his parental home for good (Oyono 13). A little further on, he writes: "My parents are dead. I have never been back to the village" (14). We shall see the disastrous consequences of this on his destiny at the end, when compared especially with that of Njoroge. The latter, as we have said, spent all his childhood with his parents.

Njoroge inherits his parents' lifelong ambition: to recover their lost land which, to his father, Ngotho, was "a spiritual loss" as well (Ngugi 74). It is mainly for this reason that he was sent to school, for, as Ngotho himself says, "education was good only because it would lead to the recover)- of the lost lands" (39). Right from the start therefore, Njoroge feels weighing on his young fragile shoulders the onerous task of playing a messianic role:

> Njoroge listened to his father. He instinctively, knew
> that an indefinable demand was being made on him,
> even though he was so young. he knew that for him

education would be the fulfilment of a wider and more significant vision a vision that embraced the demand made on him (...). He saw himself destined for something big, and this made his heart glow (Ngugi 39)

Little by little he comes to believe that God may have chosen him to be the instrument of His Divine Service" (94). Hence this prayer on hearing that he is going to go to High School: "Give me more and more learning and make me the instrument of Thy Light and Peace" (104). The budding Moses was confirmed in this vision of his national messianic role on the occasion of his departure for High School:

> Somehow the Gikuyu people always saw their deliverance as embodied in education. When the time for Njoroge to leave came near, many people contributed money so that lie could go.
> He was no longer the son of Ngotho but the son of the land (...). Njoroge had now a new feeling of pride and power for at last his way seemed clear. The land needed him and God had given him an opening so that lie might come back and save his family and the whole country (104-105)

The reader knows the disaster that put a tragic end to these dreams. The laconic manner in which the embittered child sums up his sad story:

> "I have now lost all my education, my faith and my family .... I, alone, am left" (131). His dreams now behind him, "life seemed (to him) like a big lie where

people bargained with forces that one could not see "
(126).

The hero of *Houseboy,* Toundi, for his part, is a blind
victim of these invisible forces from the very beginning of
the novel. Unlike Njoroge, all his "schooling" consists of
learning how to read and write which the white missionary
taught him with the sole aim of making him more useful as a
houseboy.

> "Father Gilbert says I can read and write fluently.
> Now I can keep a diary like he does." (Oyono 9

We know that this "diary" is actually the novel,
Houseboy. Naive and imprudent, inexperienced and deaf to
reason, Toundi commits one blunder after another,
believing stupidly all the time that he enjoys the powerful
protection of the commandant. Wasn't he "the dog of the
king," and hence the "king" among his fellow "dogs"? Who
would dare to harm the "chief European's boy?" (20).

Unlike Njoroge's, all his ambition for the future is a
purely self-centred vague seeking to become like the
white man he serves, without knowing too well how to go
about it. When, one day, the commandant's wife advises
him "to buy a wife"- flattering him that "as the
commandant's house boy he is an attractive match he
answers: "Perhaps, madam, but my wife and children will
never be able to eat and dress like madam or like white
children" (Oyono 56).

Having severed the umbilical cord that links him with
his ancestral "primitive" origin, he wants to become a
white man with black skin. Subconsciously, he thinks he
has become a member of the Decazy family hence "(he)

could do what (he) like(d)" (73) Even though he discovers the secret of the myth of the white man's "racial superiority complex": hypocrisy, he still aspires to resemble him. This infantile megalomania as madam Decazy points out to him (56), coupled with his incurable naive confidence in the commandant's all-powerful protection, blinds him to the fact the he could one day fall victim to this hypocrisy, whose universally recognized stock in trade is treachery and betrayal.

This brings us to the last point of difference between Toundi and Njoroge, the last and in the fact the greatest, as it is a matter of life and death, a question of to be or not be. "If water is polluted at its very source..." begins in Igbo proverb. Toundi's "source" [destiny] is vitiated right from his earliest childhood.

Forced by the punitive brutality of an iron-fisted father to flee his parental home, he becomes literally prisoner of his greed which attaches him irresistibly to the world of the white man.

He grows deaf to all advice and warning to flee the residence "when the water [was] still only up to the knees" i.e. before the river swallows [him] up altogether - according to the time-tested saying of our ancestors (100). A few days after this warning, to which he paid a deaf ear, he is shot and killed at the Spanish Guinea frontier in a belated attempt to escape from his fate. He had left his destiny in the hands of the white man and the latter had disposed of it as his colonialist predatory greed dictated.

Njoroge, as we have seen, goes from an optimistic vision of bright "tomorrow" to a bitter disappointment which finds hi in a situation, "to which 'tomorrow' was no longer answer. (Ngugi 122). In such a bleak predicament, he has only just one ray of hope: in love. In his love for Nwihaki, he begs the latter to escape with him from the wicked reality of their country –a disguised form of suicide. He has lost all hope in any future; but Nwihaki opposes this cowardly escapism. "She sat there, a lone tree defying darkness, trying to instil new life. in him. But he did not want to live. Not this kind of life." (133)

When Nwihaki bluntly refuses to yield to his own type of "life," his last hope vanishes with the dying steps of the retreating girl, symbolised by the last rays of "the sun (that) was sinking" (134). He sinks into total despair. Pessimism and nihilism take control of him, and his attempted suicide is not a surprise in such circumstances. But he is timely saved from putting his neck in the noose by the voice of mother, Nyokabi, calling to him out of the darkness... (135-136). Suicide is the worst form of escapism, the last and final surrender of a coward before the challenge of living is the only irreparable failure in life. Njoroge therefore "feels a strange relief to have been saved *in extremis*, and as he humbly accompanies his mother home, he feels ashamed of his triple failure:

> He followed her, saying nothing. He was only conscious that he had failed her and the last word of his father, when he had told him to look after the women. He had failed the voice of Nwihaki that had asked him to wait for a new day. (... He) felt only guilt, the guilt of a man who had avoided his responsibility for which he had prepared himself since childhood. (Ngugi 136)

Having accepted the challenge to live, he behaves true to a very wise saying of Igbo: *Kama aga amu ozum amu, si mua uzo msi gba oso* (which paraphrased in English means:

better a living coward than a dead hero). He therefore ignores the "voice" rebuking him for being "a coward" (since he had also "failed" tins "voice" too, by not committing suicide). He therefore accepts being a coward, "and ran home and opened the door for his two mothers" (136).

Conclusion

So much in common, and yet how dissimilar in the end or, are they really? All the differences between Toundi and Njoroge can be traced back to one that is fundamental: Toundi's deafness to advice and his escape from his parental home. He was like a young plant plucked from its roots and thrown on a rough river; how and where can such a plant ever take roots again? Both he and Njoroge represent Africa exploited and tortured in its infancy (we are in the pre-independence era). For, this we agree with the German philosopher, Nietzsche, who says that man's tragedy is that he was once a child, i.e. the last-comer to the adult world of scrambling humanity, and hence the victim of other' predatory greed.

But Toundi and Njoroge represent two faces of the same child Africa; one that imprudently breaks with all tradition in a naïve and blind chase after the white man's "better" way of life [this is tantamount to cultural suicide, symbolised by Toundi's death at. cross-roads between two countries]; the other which while holding solidly to tradition, seeks to acquire the white man's secret of domineering power: education. Njoroge's deliverance *in extremis* by his mother's voice is a ray of hope; telling a suffering 'and weeping Africa that "hope of a better day was the only comfort (one) could give to a weeping child"

[Ngugi 111]. Will that "better day" come with the era of independence?

Even though Oyono and Ngugi each wrote in different countries, in different languages, and in slightly different, historical circumstances, and did not know (or have to know) each other's existence, they still gave to the child, Africa, the same message in tragically different ways. This comparative study shows that *Houseboy* and *Weep not, child* are two complementary novels, and could, with great benefits, be studied as such. There is no limit to what may be discovered by undertaking such a study of any authors or even the same author.

Chapter 5

Children in a Discourse

GMT Emezue

CHILDREN'S literature in African writing still remains a shot in the dark. Few writers bother themselves in this field and even fewer critics (African) have glanced through with a view towards eliciting the merits and demerits of this genre. Thus, the terrain remains the path not trodden. Its target audience (children) may consequently become like wanderers in a literary wilderness, groping their way towards the illumination of intellect and balance of emotion. As the world inexorably rolls onward to a global township, Africa is left behind. Yet if properly appreciated, this genre remains the singular potential for shaping the future and destiny of African nations. Many 'advanced' nations that have recognised the importance of this genre and its need as a viable venture, invest a lot of financial and human resources in this area. Until then one can only hope that one day Africa may recall her children wandering in the wilderness of life.

While some writers do realise the importance and necessity of filling up the yawning gap in this area, many that dabble into this area do so purely for economic purposes. Few writers are conscious of the great onus and responsibility their 'calling' has imposed on them to produce works inspired of great spirit, such that may dramatically alter the future of our young for the better, works that could appeal to and transform the restless and inquisitive mind of a child into an unquenchable thirst for knowledge, the use of which will reshape the future of our country Nigeria. Such writers are indeed rare.

Anezi Okoro falls into this group of 'conscious artistes' with other writers along with Mabel Segun, Nkem Nwankwo, Cyprian Ekwensi, Rose Uwemedimo, and Kole Onadipe. This discussion comes after decades of silence. Some of the questions answered here by this remarkable man of our times would, hopefully, help to steer children's writing in Africa, and indeed Africa's leadership and her progeny, towards the lushness of truly inspired creativity we have always cherished.

A Writer and his Thoughts

Anezi Okoro was born in Arondizuogu. According to him, "My father was a heathen but during harvest time he will allow his wives and children to attend the church function." This way he was exposed and later converted to the Christian fold.

He left home at an early age to live with his brother who was teaching at Methodist College, Uzuakoli. It was there that he attended primary school and later secondary school after which he proceeded to read medicine at the university. Currently he is Professor of Medicine (Dermatologist) at Ebonyi State University, Abakaliki. He is married with five children.

Okoro is undoubtedly one of the pioneer writers in African Children's literature. Through thirty seven years of creative writing, Anezi Okoro has produced over 8 children stories and two works for adults. Yet his creative resources have not exhausted as we gather from the interview. To his credit are *The Village School* (1966), *The Village Headmaster* or *New Broom at Amanzu* (1967), *Febechi in Cave Adventure* (1971), *One Week One Trouble* (1973), *Down the Niger* (1974), *Dr Amadi's Postings* (1974), *Double Trouble* (1985), *Education is Great* (1986), *Pariah Earth and other stories* (1994). Among the books that are yet to be published include *The Eclipse* and *The Flying Tortoise*, among many others.

Professor Okoro was 1988 keynote speaker for Ahiajioku Lecture. His address entitled 'Chukwu ka Dibia: A look into Igbo Traditional Medicine' explored five thousand years of Igbo ethno-medicine. Among the published poems are 'Spirits of Midnight' (1989) Poetic Voices of America, 'Light' (1989) American Poetry Annual, 'The Village Drum (1989) The National Library of Poetry, 'Our Only Home' (1990), 'Desert Sand' (1990), *The Poetry Centre*, 'Around the World' (1990) The Poetry Centre, 'Lightning' (1990) The Poetry Centre, 'No More Dreams' (1990), The Poetry Centre, 'Horizon' (1991), Watermark Press, 'Forest' 1992, Watermark Press, 'Bittersweet' 1992 Watermark Press, 'Home' (1994), The National Library of Poetry, 'Useful Vulture' (1994), The National Library of Poetry, 'The Millstone Gone', (1995) Sparrowgrass Poetry Forum.

What has been your source of inspiration for your numerous novels?

A little book called *Things Worth Knowing*. This tiny book, which I saw in my elder brother's house while I was with him, made a great impression on me by the kind of knowledge it contained. This little book of some few pages contained information on general knowledge and the like. When I read it, my imagination was fired and I started reading other books. With lots of reading, I had the inclination to write. That was how I started writing.

Your children's books set in the 'school system' show a well organised educational system with dedicated teachers (even if over-zealous) unlike what we have today. Was this type of plot structure specially chosen by you or was it a reflection of the period and time you were writing?

Generally, many of my characters represent snippets of the kind of time and period I saw as a child. The kind of characters I portray where the kind of characters that existed in those days. Then, the teachers were respected. The teachers were happy to know that they were bringing up young minds. They served as role models for their pupils. There was no way teachers combined their duties with other jobs. There wasn't divided attention. There wasn't the TV (television) at that time. So as a student you pick your novel and go under a tree to read. It was so difficult for things to go wrong. It was mission schools in those days. *The Village School* and *Village Headmaster* happened in that type of school. Although I did not set out to simply record this period, yet I discovered that my characters were so representative of the period that many people who read those stories in those days say 'Oh, this is exactly, what happened in my own primary school'. So the stories represented what was general at that time.

But then speaking of education, we, in the hinterland, came in late into education, because education and

Christianity came through the coast and took some time reaching the hinterland. Once we embraced it, we went about it in a big way to get educated. So it should still be our priority because it is our passport to a good life. Other people may have other priorities, but we should ensure that education remains our priority. It may not appear to pay in the short run, but in the long run it does. Some people have made money but what is the money for? The more money you have, the more likely it becomes the money will control you. So again you don't get happiness. These kiddies books that showed a time, and a way, that things were properly done should be read more (often). Those books are not widely read now. If some people read those books and they get the kind of attention we are giving them now, I believe that things will be better. But nowadays people push in something that doesn't give any message and they get accepted. But the children suffer. My view on this is that our education system needs to be overhauled. Once sanity returns to the education system things will be better for the kids. So I hope that those children's books that show better educational system could be read more widely. But today the attention is divided in many ways. But then nothing can go right if the school system is wrong.

In The Village Headmaster *the activities of the wolf cub club seemed to be portrayed in negative light. The two accidents that occurred in the book were as a result of the activities of this group. Do you any special reason for this?*

It would be a pity if that is the impression created. I was a wolf cub. Perhaps the accidents were just accidents and ways of resolving some complications in the story without spoiling the storyline. It's just one of those things. I tried to use the accidents rather than deliberate injuring or killing.

One week one Trouble *is full of the escapades of Wilson Tagbo and in* Double Trouble *Wilson seems to have gone too far.*

Of interest is the portrayal of the Masquerade cult whose activities are supposed to be the 'cult practices that students are discouraged from engaging in.' This blurb warning seems at odds with the events in the book. For instance, Agrippa, an elder in the masquerade cult member admonishes Akidi and his young masquerade group saying: 'I still think that your methods were too cruel for our customary initiation. You will ruin our tradition if you carry on that way and I will not let you.' (p. 114)

Of course the traditional masquerade cult is not negative because they serve some purposes for their society. It's a misrepresentation. That blurb was not mine. It was inserted by my publishers probably with the aim of advertising and selling the book. Well campus cults as we know them now have no relationship between them and the traditional cults that we find in the villages.

In fact whatever is misguiding these people is best understood by them, because in American, British, Russian universities you have clubs that you might call cults. But these groups engage in social works and so on.

This is the generation for misapplications. Take the original university cults like Wole Soyinka's Pirates Confraternity, (for example) the name sounds bad, but they were known to do social work. They developed the Federal Road Safety Corps and when they ran it, they did it effectively and efficiently. So fighting, damaging and destructive cults in secondary and tertiary institutions didn't draw inspiration from the traditional masquerade society. Take some South-South States for example, the Epe society is a cult, but it is not destructive. The Ozo is a cult, and it is not destructive. Indeed you have to be noble to be accepted in these cults. But I don't see any sign of nobility in any of these cults in the tertiary institutions.

The problem here, as we once discussed at the University of Nigeria, is that of frustration and lack of recreational facilities for students. (We are looking at) a situation where you have about 15,000 able-bodied young men and women at the peak of their life with no tennis courts, badminton courts or facilities for outside activities provided for them where these excess energies could be burnt off. During our school days we didn't give out the building of recreational facilities on contract. Why wouldn't students be ready to participate in building where they will play, yes, build recreational facilities by direct labour. If our tertiary institution leaders can do this, it will stop the creation of these things that happen at midnight. Unless we create these outlets for these children, they will likely destroy themselves.

Is there a sequel to Double Trouble? *I believe that your readers will like to know what happened to Wilson Tagbo.*

The original story of Wilson Tagbo, I designed it as a book which I called 'Coming to Terms'. But one of the publishers suggested that when you spread a story over five years it becomes tedious. So I did the first one *One Week One Trouble* The second one *Double Trouble* I did it over night. Everything about it happened between Sunday evening 5.30 after service and Monday morning eight

O'clock. So I packed so many activities in those fourteen hours and *Double Trouble* came out.

I designed the story of Wilson Tagbo to come out in five books. But so far I am in Book Two that is *Double Trouble*. I would've continued it as a series just like the *Febechi* series. The third of the Febechi series has been written that is *Febechi in Eclipse*, but sadly, the publishers that did *Febechi* one and two have folded. I tried AUP (African Universities Press) to handle it, but I discovered that many publishers have fallen on hard times. May be I'll rescue it because that story is also exciting and educating. Usually that's how I have designed those books to write them and continue them in series. There are many other books in the English series that are in that way.

In some developed countries of the world, writers see creative writing as a life-long career. They may not need to work or do any other thing for a living. But in Africa such is not possible. What has your experience been like being a writer and other such professional commitments?

In the first few years I made what little I could. I don't think that I've ever made enough from all my writing to live for one month. The last royalties I received from AUP that published *Village School, Village Headmaster, One Week on Trouble, and Double Trouble,* all of which are being read, was four, five years ago. Because pirates produce these books regularly, my publishers are getting nothing and I get nothing. Pirates are getting everything.

Once, the publishers asked me what to do about the situation. I asked them how many copies of *One Week One Trouble* -we all accept that *One Week One Trouble* is the most popular in the market- they had in print. He said 'about 5,000'. But how many do you think are needed in a year? 5,000 (copies) could be consumed in Idemmili Local Government Area (in Anambra State of Nigeria) alone. If the requirement for the book in a year is about 200,000 copies and you print only 5,000 copies, where do you want the students to get the other 195,000 copies?

They were printing 5,000 copies when there were few schools. Now schools are everywhere. If they printed 200,000 copies they would still sell them even cheaper and make more money. So the pirates now print the books. It's a pity because many people believe that I ought to be rich. Since the Febechi series not a Kobo has come in 20 years. From AUP books if I am lucky every 5 or 10 years.

Writing Science Fiction

Pariah Earth and other Stories *is your most recent work. It makes an interesting reading. So far, you seem to be among the first few African writers exploring this field of science fiction in such depth and magnitude. What started you in this direction?*

As I said earlier the tiny little book which I met in my senior brother's house *Things Worth Knowing* had a lot of information concerning such things as the five continents (they believed that America was a continent then), the major capitals of the world, the great emperors, the biggest lakes, tallest mountains, just general knowledge. I was fascinated by the pyramids, the various planets and such knowledge. Since then, I have always pursued my reading wide, not narrow. Even at the medical school, I always read outside the medical field. I just enjoyed sitting down and lapping up information from encyclopaedia, journals which I subscribe to and so on. That's how I picked up astronomy and other things. So that was how my curiosity was awakened and because I read wide, I can write on any subject I chose.

I like the book too, that is *Pariah Earth and Other Stories*. Although I feel that people will find the first story very dry. You know, you have to know about the constellation and the solar system to enjoy the story. In the story I tried to give character to the various planets. At the time the book came out a Ghanaian friend of mine said 'You know that if you had put 'Great Flood II' first people can understand the book' But there is another book that is coming out before the year runs out -The *Flying Tortoise*. I believe that people might find this one less 'technical'. In the story I used the story of tortoise, the mythology of tortoise to teach children astronomy, the different planets, the stars and so on. I invented a reason that will make him fly. So it flew. The book is set for children, unlike *Pariah Earth*, which is not for children, although young adults or juveniles can read with ease and enjoyment.

The way the plot of Pariah Earth *was going one would be tempted to conclude that Earth would be destroyed and Mars punished. But rather Sun came in to make a case for Earth. Why was this twist necessary?*

Super-intelligence. What else? Although we recognize the fact that the more primitive you are the less destructive, yet we all yearn for development. The more you migrate the more you develop because if you ask (yourself) why have we developed least? You will discover that when the super continent (that is all the five continents in the world were together). Then man started migrating from East Africa from where man evolved (not created).

93

You'd discover that the farther you migrate, the more you develop. Those who migrated to Asia and other European countries, see their rate of development. But my argument is that the farther away from home you go the greater the likelihood of challenges therefore the more you will struggle to survive. I'll give you an example with my hometown. From my hometown, the richest people were the people who went to other lands and places to settle. We are the least developed because we migrated least from East Africa.

Compared with your previous writings, what do you think of science fiction as a creative output?

I enjoy both types of writing. If I had time I would've liked to write more. But right now, I come out to work, see patients, teach the medical students, go home, and squeeze in a little time in my writing, (and) rest. I intend to write many more books. People might say, here is a man in his seventies talking of writing many more books, but why not? I will. It is the debt we owe including you. Our parents who couldn't write left us oral history in those days.

Those of us who can write, we owe a lot. It's a debt. It almost with the fervour of politics that I am stressing that we should write. Because the Caucasian world and other countries will think that we have made no contribution to knowledge if we don't. When there was no writing, we couldn't be blamed. But now that we can write, we'll just have to write and write and write. We must write in as many languages as we can. I write in Igbo. Sometimes I say to myself that I've written so many books in English, I have to write in Igbo and I do it. It is a disgrace that whereas other major and even not so major ethnic groups in Nigeria uphold their languages, we are dropping our own completely. We speak Hausa happily, we speak Yoruba, but we don't speak Igbo, we don't even write in it. We owe it as a debt. All of us should write and write and write. Don't look at the money yet, just write and write. It is the debt we owe.

The environment of all the stories (except two) in Pariah Earth and other Stories *are outside the African continent. Don't you think it beclouds the authenticity of this book as truly African literature?*

No. I don't think so. To start with events in those stories, 'Pariah Earth', 'Great Flood II' are global events. For instance when the great flood takes place, which shall be soon, because the Antarctica and Arctic ice are breaking up due to increase in temperature all around the world, it's going to affect everybody in the world. So it will not be possible to set such events in one corner of the world. Africa is well documented in the story. For instance, the name Iyk, which is the name the hero bears, is an Igbo name. Also the site chosen for studies in final rescue operations and re-establishment of the earth is Mt. Kilimanjaro in Tanzania. This is in Africa, although it is primarily chosen because it is the tallest mountain in the world and might probably be the last to be affected by great flood II. Well it just happened that the settings and characters appear that way. But when you see *Flying Tortoise* such issues won't come up because it's purely African, both in setting and characterization.

All the characters in the 'Great Flood II' *are of mixed races. Do you foresee a future possibility of this and what would be its advantage?*

We are a fast moving world, people are blending and intermarrying. Although I don't foresee a future where everybody will be of mixed races, but there is going to be a lot of mixing up alright. The characters in my book reveal such a future and possibility, alright, because it is already happening. The Ozone layer is breaking up and global warming is already taking place. When we talk of one world, it shall not only be in environment alone, you will also discover that most people are related to each other. I write about all these simply to make people aware of the danger of destroying our environment with toxic waste, CFC, bush burning and the like.

How has critical reception of your works been both within and outside Nigeria?

There's been little or no mention of my books in the critics' circle. The books are available and some of them are over thirty years old. Perhaps the critics don't rate them as highly as you do, because you've seen them all. A writer doesn't have to write just for critics. When I wrote *One week One Trouble*, I wanted it published in Heinemann (Nigeria Ltd.). A Nigerian reviewer felt that the book is too English; that the narrative is too flat and there is nothing African in it. He doesn't think that anyone will read it. So eventually I took it back and when I sent it to this publisher (African University Press) and they brought it out, you need to see the way it is going. You need to see how our young girls fell in love with Wilson Tagbo. They would meet me and say 'We like that boy- o'

So you can only play your own part and maybe the critics, in the course of time, will play their own part. But then if you look at our international writers like Chinua Achebe; who were the people that brought him to limelight? Is it African critics? No. It was European critics. (For) Wole Soyinka (it was) the same thing. So maybe I shall be patient until I get outsiders interested in my work. Until then my purpose is just to write.

Pariah Earth and other stories was published overseas. I happened to be out of the country by then. But again, the publishers did not promote it enough. Perhaps at the back of their mind could be this thing you said, you know, whether an African should be writing scientific stuff. I don't have a chip on my shoulder about colour or anything like that. I never had, because I have always believed that superiority or inferiority is here (*pointing to the head*). But I suspect that the people after recommending it highly had a pang of colonial mentality after they published it. Because the effort they made to promote the book was nil. Indeed, at a point, I directed them to the World Conference on Environment of 1996. I suggested they send copies of the book to this conference, but they did not do anything of the sort. If they had sent the books to this conference, perhaps the book would have had a better outing. Then in Berlin, two years later another conference on Environment took place, followed by another one in Tokyo, Japan. On both occasions, I alerted the publishers, but they did not do anything. I just said well, this might be a colonial thing. They did not expect an African to know something about such things, how much more daring to write about such things. I mean 'how dare he?'

Is there any hope of publishing this work in Nigeria or any African country?

I might likely contemplate publishing the book in Nigeria. The company that took over the other publishing company abroad wrote to me and said, 'What do you want us to do with your work?" I replied them but I haven't got any response. But whatever it is I have the copyright.

There has been a change in focus in publishing. Many publishers demand full payment for the printed work from the author. How has this affected your writing and your works?

Actually, it has limited the number of works that I would have published within a given time. But it doesn't stop me from writing. If I had time I will like to write more. If I were properly retired, perhaps, then I would have devoted more time to my writing. Although I would be bored if I stayed at home just writing. So I manage to put in time for my writing when I return from the office.

On The Debt We Owe

You were quoted in 20th century Children's Writers edited by Tracy Chevalier, along with other writers like Chinua Achebe and Cyprian Ekwensi. The book is all about writers of children's literature all over the world. Nigeria is among the countries with the least writers. It must be observed that Children's literature is not widely read or appreciated in Africa. One wonders why it is so. Is it because of the child-heroes that appear in these works or the readership we have?

Look at our schools nowadays. Who bothers about reading? The pupils and students read only what is compulsory. Tell me what is compulsory in schools? The reading culture is dying. (The) radio and television will not allow children to read. When I was growing up, there was no radio, no television anywhere. You pick a novel, go under a big tree and you relax and read. But it is not like that now. So the reading culture needs to be created.

In the field of writing, sometimes we just write. Somehow some adults write for adults, and some superior adults write for superior adult who read things their own level. They say educate a man, you educate an individual, educate a woman, you educate a family. When you write for adults, you write only for an individual, the scope is limited but when you write or children, you write for the nation, for the future So that's the debt we owe. I think we should make greater effort in this direction.

As I said earlier, I didn't kind of design it, but I just like lapping up general knowledge, but since I saw the general picture -that we don't write enough for children and the little that is written is not accessible. Since I saw the critical nature of the situation (which you have also seen) I have made it my area of focus. The few of us who recognize the need for our children to read should try to write. It is what we need to do for our children. The few who aspire to write should write for children. We should make our children realize the importance of reading. I think that the few of us who recognize the need to write for our children need to do a lot of work in this direction.

We don't have to write big. If we look around (we can see the) trees, flowers, observing things. That's what we need to do for our children. And if we can concentrate I believe that we can solve the problem. I tell you this little book got me inspired as a child. Other well-written books can also be of keen interest for other children. I have coming out soon, a series of children's poetry entitled 'Verses for the Young' but I changed it to *Ringing Verses for African Children 1,2,3.* In it I have such poems as the following:

> See the new moon like a C See the half moon like a D
> See the full moon like a big big O...

The Vulture

> Poor old Vulture Has no Culture Eats dead rat That's
> the reason Every Season
> It looks old, and sick and sad...

A child who cries

> A child who cries Will have sore eyes And wrinkled
> nose And funny toes ...

As you rightly observed the movie culture development has contributed to the dwindling of the reading culture. Unfortunately this culture has come to stay, but there is something the Caucasian world has done. They have serials of notable adventure stories of their great writers. I am of the opinion that someone like Wilson Tagbo might be a great influence on the kids. Personally, I was inspired by this genius, though a rascal, who committed so many atrocities in the school but made very high grades in school. If you have an opportunity to have this book on celluloid, would you envisage some trouble in terms of copyright?

I think that it would be a great development. Say for instance, if you watch the film, you will like to read the book. If you've read the book, you will like to watch the film. I am for anything that will stimulate reading in the youths.

When Harold Macmillan visited Nigeria, I was running a class called writers and readers club of Nigeria. He became a member of our club. The club thrived for some time. We certainly have to find ways to take care of our reading problems here, because we couldn't tell the world to stop we want to get out. The late Victor Nwankwo was my model. He went to the extent of putting my book, an Igbo translation of Shakespeare stories, on internet so that anyone that wants the book can download it. Such ideas help develop our reading culture along the trends of the new world order. So this idea you speak of is a good one, since it will help promote reading.

War and concerns for the future

You were you in Nigeria during the Nigeria civil war; how did that affect you as a writer?

Point of correction, I wasn't in Nigeria; I was in Biafra during the war. Actually I did some writing then. This series of ringing verses were written almost all the time of Biafra. But I also have my story on war. It is a novel, which ran into 600 pages. But I just dumped it there. Perhaps I might brush it up and decide to publish it later on. But right now I am occupied with other works.

What might you be working on at the moment?

As I said earlier, I expected a lot of book harvest this year. But unfortunately it has not come through as I planned. But then they might all be out by 2003. 'Double Thrilling' is a critique of the 6-3-3-4 system of education. It is something I am working on. This idea of making the secondary school blend into university and not allowing a gap like all countries do is causing a lot of problems for us in this country. You can't imagine that the O' Level result is not yet out and every SS3 child is rushing off to take JAMB. Now if you see scores some people make in JAMB you know that they ought not to aim for higher education in a tertiary institution.   All other countries of the world like Russia, India, Japan, and America, all recognize O' Level as endpoint of Secondary education. But Nigeria is the exception.

Many of the disaster, armed robbery and violence that bedevil our country at the moment are partly because everybody is hurrying to university, when everybody is not made for university. But in Nigeria if you insist that people must get their basic qualifications first before proceeding further academically, the Northerners will tell you that it is because you know that it is only the southerners that will pass, that is why you are insisting on their being edged out educationally. So we allow everybody to take JAMB. But if JAMB will be kind enough to publish every child's result and send to the parents, it will open our eyes to what is happening. Because everybody takes JAMB and the next thing you hear is 'JAMB didn't favour me.' If we really think of those things, expand our vision such that we can stop students from using other people to take their exams for them for example, it will help our country. So this book I am talking about is concerned with such problems and their consequences.

Chapter 6

Hearts *and* Ballads

P. Onwudinjo

THEMES of political consciousness are the most dominant and recurrent in contemporary Nigerian poetry. Such themes aimed at arousing the consciousness of the Nigerian masses to the political condition of their nation have continued to engage the attention of many contemporary Nigerian poets. This fact is attested to by the number of Nigerian poets who devote large proportions of their work to the exploration of national and political issues. This appraisal analyses the various forms through which political consciousness is expressed in Ada Ugah's *Naked Hearts* (1982) and *Ballad of the Unknown Soldier* (1989).

Like many Nigerian poets such as Odia Ofeimun, Niyi Osundare, Ezcnwa-Ohaeto, Chinweizu, Femi Fatoba etc, Ada Ugah grapples with the vices that frustrate the democratic process and threaten the political stability of Nigeria. Like many of his colleagues too, he is committed, both in the content and form of his poetry, to the exploration of problems contingent on Nigeria's post-war situation. The recurrent failure of the democratic system and the burdensome presence of military interregnum politically crippled Nigeria for twenty-eight out of her forty-two years of existence as a nation.

Ada Ugah's poetry reveal the writer's deep-seated sympathy for, and total commitment to the poor and deprived masses of African nations who bear the brunt of military despotism and civil misgovernance. His creative impulse is consistency toward the expression of the socio-political contradictions that impoverish the Nigerian polity.

In the poem entitled 'Interlude,' Ada Ugah endorses Odia Ofeimun's observation that 'the guilty are too well-fed to pass /through the needle's eye of our scorn' (8). The simplicity of his diction and the clarity of his voice seek the larger audience beyond the ivory tower. In a poem entitled "The Poet Wails," Ada Ugah condemns the naked greed he spies behind the manoeuvre of many Nigerian politicians, and holds that:

> Behind cascades
> of ancestral plumes
> Ogre skulks in nudity (92)

This remark foreshadows his mythic exploration of the ogre in *Ballads of the Unknown Soldier* published in 1989, seven years after *Naked Hearts*. The Ballads, a work conceived as fiction and expressed in poetry, evokes a nightmarish mythic event in which a man metamorphoses into a serpent and blocks the route of social intercourse in Nigeria. Ugah expresses disgust over the recurrent abuse of power by both civilian and military leaders by casting such leaders in the image of predators. He castigates corrupt politicians for 'preying on the masses,' and 'fat-feeding with language of democracy' (92). These are the discredited politicians of the first and the second Nigerian Republics who used their powerful financial muscles to elbow themselves into the seat of power through vote-buying. Ada Ugah's fellow poets and colleagues have also addressed themselves to the twin vices of insincerity and empty promises. Niyi Osundare condemns the-

> Organised grins
> Made up cheers (and) Rehearsed grins (23)

of the typical Nigerian. And Catherine Acholonu expresses a vehement rejection of the politicians' 'ala carte smiles, handshakes, grins of satisfaction' (70). Their mannerisms and faked bonhomie evoked in these poems echo strongly the boisterous laughter and larger-than-life postures of Chief Nanga in Chinua Achebe's novel: *A Man of the People*. These poems expose the extravagant and insincere life styles typical of Nigerian politicians in the first Republic and adopted by their successors in second democratic experiment who did not seem to have learnt anything from the collapse of the undemocratic politics of the first regime. Ugah showcases senators who invent high-sounding schemes aimed at attracting government-sponsored trip abroad. They are

> Tourist senators (who)
> Window-shop in Warsaw
> And holiday
> In air-birds
> On legislative tours (92)

Here the poet's reflection of the Nigerian political condition is so close to reality that the boundary between the two becomes fluid. During the second Republic, some members of the federal house were actually sent on a working tour of the United States of America to study the American system of presidential democracy. Such avoidable expenditure was part of the economic mismanagement that left Nigeria with virtually empty coffers and necessitated the crippling devaluation of the Naira. The poet sees his art as a way of awakening the consciousness of the masses to the dangers posed to society by these human predators in leadership positions.

Like most other younger Nigerian poets, Ada Ugah does not hide his total disenchantment with the leadership in Nigeria; nor does he cease

> To wail with the masses.... (and)
> To weep with the toads of society (93).

Ada Ugah's perception of the problem of political corruption is sympathetic towards the uniformed masses who, perhaps out of ignorance or greed, or maybe ethnic sentiments, make themselves easy prey for exploitative politics. Nigeria's older writers such as Chinua Achebe and Wole Soyinka had blame both politicians and electorate for the failure of democracy in Nigeria, and in fact accuse the Nigerian polity of 'having led the politicians on' to the failure of Nigeria's first and second Republics. But Ada Ugah unequivocally takes sides with the masses, the major victims of political failures. His poems affirm his faith in the ability of the deprived and exploited to grapple with the problems and eventually transform society. The poem entitled 'The poet wails' is a call for workers' solidarity against a repressive system. In this poem too, his solidarity with the masses is obvious, for, the poet says:

> On May day
> Dawn crier cried
> With Talakawa
> The poet cried (93)

The poet continues his defence of the deprived in 'Dance of the Purdah Woman,' claiming that despite Muslim argument to the contrary, the system of confining women in a harem is repression of women's rights and deprivation of the individual freedom of movement and association. The poem is a metaphor of various other types of deprivations and violations of basic human rights, particularly women's rights.

'Dance of the Missing Jungle' shows abuse of power and authority. The poem is in the form of a dialogue between 'drummers' and 'moon dancers' (96). The poet protagonist dons the image of a village drummer and announces his mission:

> I drum for the man
> Who uses official vehicle for private use
> I drum for that army officer
> Who abandons troop salaries in the bank
> (for) the labour leader
> Who gets some 'dash' to hoodwink the congress
> ....for assemblymen
> who abandon employment to award "self salaries' (96).

These allusions are everyday occurrences in the Nigerian society. The misuse of official vehicles is so wide-spread now that it has virtually ceased to be regarded as an offence against the law to put government vehicles to personal use. The poet is attacks this abuse of power, which was very rampant during the Second Republic, a period of the infamous winner-takes-all syndrome when politicians and every wielder of the littlest power constituted themselves into demi-gods. But the acid rain of the worst abuse of power came crashing down on Nigeria during the military regimes that followed.

The 'Moon dancers' announce that they are dancing 'for common liberty,' 'for social justice,' 'for social liberation,' 'for change of society,' 'for an end of exploitation,' and 'for a better day.'(96) But theirs is not a dance of joy. It is a dance of anger provoked by the pain of 'our missing jungle ... Our missing oil boom.' (97) The poems reflect the poet's disgust with the regrettable governance of the country under a hegemony that demonstrated an unimaginable capacity for wasteful expenditure and political irresponsibility.

The poet pursues the theme of political irresponsibility and reckless waste of public funds in 'Dance of the Missing Jungle.' Ugah's titles are symbolic. The jungle has been the friend of man since the dawn of mankind. It is the source of food for man before he learnt to cultivate the soil. The forest provides shelter from weather and predators. Both in Africa and the Americas, the jungle offered refuge to slaves fleeing from their oppressors. Above all, the jungle is the only assurance that the earth will not go naked and unprotected from the vagaries of weather and climate, or starved 'of oxygen which green plants release into the atmosphere during the day. The actual and the symbolic importance of the jungle therefore make it an appropriate image for describing the wealth of the nation. In 'Dance of the Missing Jungle,' the poet grapples with Nigeria's refractory disease of financial mismanagement. In 'Dance of Disabled Falcons,' a poem subtitled after J. P. Clark's "Casualties," the poet expresses his perception of the truly disabled of the Nigerian society. He argues that 'the disabled are not the inmates of Uturu Hopeville,' nor are they 'the one-fingered lepers of Uzuakoli,' that they are neither 'the victims of natural disasters,' nor 'the denizens of the troubled land of Zion' (99). He contends that the disabled ...are those who won by two-third majority

> And (whose)... brothers became emergency
> Contractors.

They are those who lost by one-third minority and possess only three hundred and sixty plots. These disabled politicians are the types described by Niyi Osundare as:

> Power hunters wallowing through wiles
> To a minus throne-
> Cooking up numbers for a gullible mass (19).

They are the type of corrupt politicians that Catherine Acholonu accuses of conjuring 'ten plus ten to obtain two hundred thousand' (65). The disabled of Ugah's perception are the corrupt and avaricious politicians who abandoned their responsibilities to their constituencies as soon as they were elected into power. Such are disabled because their conscience is dead. They suffer a spiritual disability which has a somatic on the Nigeria polity. They are

> The colonies of...
> pot-bellied assembly men
> who tour the world capital
> neglecting their constituencies (99).

Globe-trotting and junketing are some of the vices of many Nigerian top politicians and bureaucrats, even in the first Republic. Wole Soyinka satirises this impulse to frivolity in *The Interpreters* where Chief Winsala and Sir Dorinola frivolously spend public funds acquiring various types of junk from their tours abroad. That was in 1976 when *The Interpreters* was published. More than two decades after Soyinka's satire, the globe-trotting syndrome remains a refractory disease of Nigerian military and civilian politicians.

This same impulse to globetrotting was one of the charges brought against the incumbent president Olusegun Obasanjo and from which he narrowly escaped impeachment. The search for responsible leadership in Nigeria has directly or indirectly been a major theme in contemporary Nigerian literature.

In 'Dance at Murtala Martyrdom,' (100) Ugah reconstructs the image of the late head of state, Murtala Mohammed, in heroic proportions. The poem highlights those qualities which mark Murtala Mohammed out as a national hero. Ugah's Moondancers celebrate Murtala 'the leader who battled for unity' (100). General Murtala Mohammed is generally acclaimed a national hero not because of any spectacular achievement as field commander but due to his unprecedented effort to rid the Nigerian nation of corruption and restore moral probity. Since 1976 when he fell by the assassin's bullet in an abortive coup, Nigerian writers have never failed to surround him with the halo of a martyr. Thus Ada Ugah's search for the ideal leader, a national hero is reflected in the heroic proportions in which he depicts the courageous general whose effort at national reformation was brilliant but short-lived. The poet continues his search for the leader in his *Ballads of the Unknown Soldier*.

In this experimental work conceived as prose and expressed in poetry, Ada Ugah moves away from the frontal attack that most avant garde poets make on the leaders of the Nigerian nation. 'Ballads' is a metaphor of exemplary leadership. It moves away from the well-trodden but wearisome approach of screaming at governance and presents a pleasant surprise in the myth and metaphor of the type of courage, commitment, and wisdom that it takes to be a great leader.

'Ballads' is a celebration of 'the epic combat/of man against destiny.' In his fascinating game of creative art, Ugah confronts his soldier-hero, Patrick Eje Oiji, with the mind-boggling chaos engendered by Nigeria's existential condition. This existential chaos materialises in the form of a man-turned python which bars the highway between the towns of llorin and Ogbomosho and makes social impulse impossible. Impelled by Ogun-like impulse, Patrick Eje hauls himself against this giant serpent in a titanic struggle on which the destiny of the nation hangs. Through his physical prowess and more by resorting to 'the mysteries of my land,' and 'the words of my ancestor,' the hero outwits and strangles the mysterious master, thereby restoring social and political harmony in the country.

The hero overcomes the Silurian monster by his at-oneness with the wisdom of the land. By stressing on 'the mysteries of my land,' the author affirms his faith in the spiritual resources of the Nigerian nation, and the crucial importance of those resources for national survival.

'Ballads' reflects the author's heightened perception of leadership role and sense of nationhood in a developing country. Ugah's notion of the leader is that of one who 'unlike others... refused to wait on the highway' while 'a lake of mysteries,' 'a raging flood' drives a permanent wedge between the people of Nigeria and keeps them on 'a forlorn wait' for unification. The 'lake of mysteries' (98), 'the raging floods (98), the 'floods of swollen river-flow/on man! No being ever can cross,' (91), the 'giant python/flames from its mouth' are the numerous political crises attendant on the Nigerian condition since independence.

While Eje's heroic victory casts a glance at Nigeria's victory over national disintegration, it looks forward to monumental achievements that the nation can make given committed and selfless leadership such as the hero has demonstrated. Eje's spectacular victory over the mysterious anaconda, and the national significance of that victory, makes him a national mythic hero. He ranks with other mythic heroes whose actions changed the destiny of their nations such as Sundiata, the magnificent emperor of ancient Mali; David who vanquished the giant Goliath and saved his nation from defeat and shame; Beowulf the valiant who slew the monster, Grendel; Ogun the warrior who cleared the primordial forests that separated the gods from mankind; and Bayagidda who slew the mysterious serpent that barred the way to the ancient well of Daura.

The mythic level at which Ada Ugah explores his perception of the leader reflects his level of political consciousness. In the section of Ballads entitled "Ballad of the Fortune Teller,' a diviner-protagonist looks into the future and foretells the fortunes of the hero. He enjoins the hero to 'bring Apa fame not destruction' (26). He urges the hero to 'listen to Ochekwu's injunction (26). In other words, poet envisions a national leader who will maintain healthy interaction and constant consultation with the Nigerian polity not a visiting potentate who, as Niyi Osundare describes, is surrounded by

> A clangourous convoy
> Of powers and power brokers
> Conditioned in Mercedes back
> Far, very far, from the maddening crowd (21)

-and shielded from the misery of the people. Ugah envisions a leader as a bringer of fame, not misery to his people. 'Ballads of the Fortune Teller' is a call to national reconciliation. The poet admonishes the nation:

> Let's forgo this earth's pains
> For a smile of new harvests, (28)

A joyful harvest of national reconciliation in which, to borrow General Gowon's slogan, there is 'no victor, no vanquished.'

Many of the evocations of the fortune teller look forward to a glorious dawn. In poem (xii) of 'Ballad of Fortune teller,' the poet sustains the heroic tone of his expression. In an exultant tone that echoes the psalms, he cries out:

> Oh! Night lift your veil
> Blow bugles of dawn presages
> Usher in the bridgehead

To this genteel effluvia of chronologues (35).

It is an effluvia of chronologues that command even
the attention of cosmic elements. In poem xviii of the same
ballad, the poet reflects on the problem of leadership in
Nigeria. He laments a political situation that advocates
mediocrity an unfortunate situation where 'clowns are
clowns/even with a crown (41).' The poet laments the
failed promise of the young nation, and regrets that

> This land .....
> A land of once vibrant verdure
> (is) now at stillbirth (46)

Images of stillbirth, defeated expectations,
and disillusionment and decay are recurrent in poems that
express the political condition of the Nigerian nation: In a
poem entitled 'Our Model Democracy,' Odia Ofeium laments
that

> In our model democracy
> The magic promises of yesterday
> Lie cold like mounds of dead cattle
> Along caravans that lead nowhere (4)

The 'magic promises of yesterday' that today 'lie cold
like mounds of dead cattle,' and the land of 'one vibrant
verdure/now at stillbirth' allude to the decadent political
and economic situation into which Nigeria, has fallen
since the early 1980's when the military took a second
strangle hold on Nigeria, that loosened with the sudden
demise of Abacha in 1998. Ugah attributes Nigeria's

political and economic problems to the ruinous activities of

> A protocol retinue
> Of yes men
> Of early morning do-gooders
> Still-walking as advisers! (47).

This statement is reference to the numerous special advisers, special friends, Mafioso, power brokers, and crawlers of the corridors of power who wield considerable influence over the decisions of the head of state, whether civilian or military.

Emeka Odumegwu-Ojukwu in *Because 1 Am Involved* (1989) makes an insightful analysis of the rise of sycophancy in Nigerian political practice. He holds that sycophancy is inevitable in a country like Nigeria where politics is used as an instrument for the 'castration of opposition,' and where

> Whoever controlled the Nigerian government
> Could nor only do himself and his Ilk infinite good
> (but) could also Do his opponents ... and those he
> Perceives as his opponent infinite harm. (29-30).

In poem xxxiv of 'Ballad of the Fortune Teller,' Ugah turns his attention on the problem of misgovernment in the country. The target of his attack seems to be the military establishment that established itself as a ruling class in Nigeria for more than twenty five years. He uses the metaphor of falcons swooping down on defenceless chicken to condemn the excesses of the military interregnum that has all but become a permanent feature of Nigeria politics. The poet refers to the military when he says:

> I see falcons descend on roosters
> I see them all hooded in carnation colour
> I wail for them who trained as hunters
> But now haunt the climes of our neighbourhood.

Those 'who trained as hunters but now haunt the climes of our neighbourhood' refer to the military regimes that forced their way into power and therefore did not seem to want to go back to the barracks and fully assume their primary role of defending the nation against external aggression. Having ruled Nigeria for more than two-thirds of its existence as a nation, the military lost sight of the messianic posture it adopted upon bulldozing itself into power. The discomforting presence of the military made Nigerians a captive nation. A situation where the polity is subject to the whims and caprices of a military dictatorship that owes its 'mandate' to the muzzle of the gun the image of falcons swooping down on defenceless chicken is very apt. Ugah's poetry reveals the mind of artiste concerned about the dilemmas of his country.

In 'Ballad of Ochekwu' and 'Ballad of the New Cocoa Farmer,' Ugah's consciousness of the condition of the nation takes the form of consolatory remarks and sustained celebration of the beauty of the and the unity and greatness the poet envisages for Nigeria. The 'Ballads of the Fortune Teller' rings with the hopefulness of Isaiah's prophesies: The fortune teller admonishes-

> Despair not (for)
> Life rebuilds under my shelter

I am the confluence of all rivers
The daylight is all over you (56).

Here the poet affirms his faith in the eventual recovery of
the Nigerian nation from her political and socio-
economic ills. Ugah portrays the Nigerian landscape
with such glorious colours as can only grow out of a
heart that appreciates the beauty and harmony in the
seeming chaos of nature, a heart that feels the beauty of the
country. He celebrates the beauty of

The landscape all lined
With tropical mango trees
The singing serenity
Of the open savannah grassland
And the protective mahogany canopy
And all the remaining splendour
Of nature's fulsome blooms (62).

Ugah's vision of' the chorus of nature's harmony'

Palm trees
Date palms
Coconut trees
Eaves and thatched eaves
All spaced out in azure skyline (64)

are captivating evocations of the beauty of the land. These
evocations are not fortuitous. The poet uses them to show
that a land that holds such natural beauty and harmony
should also have social and political harmony. His

concern for national unity is encapsulated in 'The Ballad of the New Cocoa Farmer' where he expresses his vision of solid national integration. When the poet says-

> North we take roots
> From the South. Our generation
> Rests in the West. Home is
> East. Omnibus
> We are the centre, (71)

he envisions a truly one Nigeria where all Nigerian citizens feel at home and arc free to exercise their rights of citizenship irrespective of place of origin/ or domicile. The poem is an oblique indictment on the divisive politics of 'North for the North' East for the East, West for the west, and Nigeria for us all.' Ugah's vision of Nigeria is a pot-pourri of nationals who have obliterated from their minds the pernicious boundaries of ethnicity, regionalism, statism, clannishness, hatred, jealousy, rancour and all forms of sectionalism and violence. The poet looks into the future of this country and sees Nigerians who have accepted themselves first and foremost as Nigerians and for whom the North is as much a home as the East or the West.

The poet describes this level of social integration as 'bliss of oneness.' He insists that only this level of unity can stop the 'heavy rain-drops/that cut instant gullies in our memory, (83) to 'the anomic season/... the era of mass self-slaughter/... the season of fratricidal fury' (84) when 'war drums were beaten night and day' (85).

By creating a mythic hero Eje, Ada Ugah implies that the solution to Nigeria's 'anomie season' depends on the emergence of leaders that have the patriotic spirit of Eje. Ada Ugah's example therefore reflects his deep understanding of human psychology. By creating an epic hero who stands as a shining example to aspiring leaders, and to all Nigerians' Ugah has gone a step ahead of the common approach of pouring vitriol on failed leaders of the country. He has marked a new direction in the growth of African poetics. His exploration of creative symbols falls in line with Bernard Haring's insistence that

> humanity needs the genius of great artists who have special grasp of the symbol, of the archetypes and cultural symbols, And can bring them home to our senses, our imagination, and Our minds in a holistic experience. (128)

Ballads of the Unknown Soldier is that kind of experience. It disengages the reader's mind from the violent metaphors common with younger Nigerian poets and presents a creative and uplifting experience. Ugah's creative bent in Ballads is not just highly entertaining; it is truly therapeutic.

Chapter 7

Njange Wan

F. Mbunda

PERFORMANCE like all other speech acts, is a communication system in which social discourse takes place principally between a narrator/performer and an audience. Malinowski in his study of Trobiad oral narratives was struck by how much was lost in the reduction of the oral text to print and the subsequent analysis of the material divorced from the context that gave it life. As Ben-Amos observes: "an oral poem is essentially an ephemeral work of art and has no existence or continuity apart from its performance" (18). Coffin and Cohening also point out that "folklore enters a state of suspended animation when in print; it becomes alive again only when it flows back into oral circulation through performance" (xiv). One gets a meaningful understanding and a deeper appreciation of Njange Wan more by observing the artists perform than by reading the texts. Finnegan asserts: "The nature of performance itself can make an important contribution to the impact of the particular literary form being exhibited" (93).

Njange Wan is context-bound. The songs have their integrity, impact and realisation only within the scope of performance, which is done on specific occasion. Malinowski makes an apt observation which is appropriate to Njange Wan:

> The text, of course, is extremely important, but without the context it remains lifeless... The whole nature of the performance, the voice and the mimicry, the stimulus and the response of the audience means as much to the natives as the text;... the performance has to be placed in its proper time setting -the hour of the day, and the season (24)

Nketia, also emphasises that "it is important to keep in mind the actual context or situation in which particular texts arc used because style, form, subject matter and meaning arc also governed by this" (28). As a cultural expression, therefore, Njange Wan is rarely analysed independently of the social context; for it is the social context that gives it an immediate application of meaning.

When a first child is born in Oku, the first woman to learn of the birth raises a jubilant alarm called "Iyaluke Wan" (joy for a child). This instantly brings other women to the scene of the delivery. This jubilant ululation is half-sung and half-chanted in high pitched tone. It is made up of gibberish syllables admixed with meaningful expressions which tell the women who has been delivered of a child, the sex of the child and where the child is born. Iyaluke Wan could be done in the hospital immediately a birth is announced or at home on the day the baby is brought home from the hospital. When the women arrive at the scene of Iyaluke Wan they begin to perform birth songs in a circular motion. It could last an hour or more, depending on the number of women who have gathered and the ability of the husband or wife's family to provide instant entertainment. As the earliest callers leave, they tend to be replaced by new ones. The purpose of this ululation is to alert the family members and get them ready to perform birth celebration, and to give publicity to the birth, and put the community in a happy mood for the celebration which the happy event always brings along with it. An example of a birth ululation runs thus:

Solo:
Ece eee eh mbofojo eee Mbofejo- ee me mboye e Chui lu iyzhio ee
Baa ee me mboye ec Mih kil fiake keghoo ee Eh gha ee ee?
Wil ah ne kebam ebkaa ee
Wil ah ne beiy ee
Wil ah ne kebam fengwange
Me mboye ee eh mbofejoe

Translation

Eee ee eh freedom ee Freedom ee I am free ee A Lion ee I am free ee
Maih has a cutlass in hand ee
Where ee? At Tolon ee
He who has money, bring it
He who has camwood, bring it
1 am free, freedom ee

From this ululation the immediate community learns that Maih has been delivered of a male child (a cutlass) at Tolon. The community is implored to bring gifts like salt, camwood and money with which to honour the baby's mother. The atmosphere of Njange Wan is informal. So the spectators come and go at will. The setting can be any place suitable for collective activity. It could be a public place like the hospital, or a private place like the home of the woman who has delivered of the baby. Most often Njange Wan is performed indoors; even in the hospital, there is a room reserved for Iyzhie Wan (birth celebration). When the first child is born, either the house of its mother or that of her mate is evacuated and reserved as "ndaa wan" (the child's house). Njange Wan takes place in this house.

At times, there are no dancing in the courtyard but it is not as prevalent as dancing indoors. Usually there are no decorations in the house. The audience can either sit or stand. Whatever the setting, the focus is on Njange Wan as one that emphasises artistic as well as social values. Njange Wan is essentially a vocal performance accompanied with dancing but never with musical instrumentation. The main elements of the performance of Njange Wan are song, dance, the performer and the audience.

The Song

The production of musical tones by means of the human voice is the oldest form of music. Singing is one of the main components of the performance of Njange Wan. The vocal techniques are based on the antiphonal exchange between the soloist (leader) and the chorus (members of the performing group). The pattern of singing includes solo and chorus alternations and the solo and chorused refrain. In this light, the chorus sings in refrain which is continuously repeated, or it could repeat the whole verse of a song after the soloist below:

Solo:
Kenue Kejunge gan me sn
Ebmbih wum momen ebwal wan

Chorus: (Repeats)

Solo:
Me shi ebvie, ne lun wun koonge me
Me mboy men e e

Chorus: (Repeats)

Solo:
Bai weh chia kuula
Jofe ka ebfua ebjunge

Chorus: (Repeats)

Translation:

Come and see
luck has come to me
My thing has tasted
a baby's excrement

I am now a woman;
I have my husband's love

Father you are more
than a leopard
More than the beauteous one

There is no permanent lead singer. Any member of the performance group can put a stop to a song by launching into the ululation of birth after which she may decide to lead. This is only when singing has readied a climax. Identical themes are repeated with different turns of phrases to achieve a great effect. For instance, the name and attributes of the woman and child are worked into appropriate places in order to create the desired impact:

Tonge nde Iyful ka Tata e e

Ishas eyum oh e e e
Eh shike kejang eh tohse iykul e e
ofe kejang ke nyime ndaa
O O Tata weh beih weh chokse ngezine

Tonge nde iykful ka kewaih e e

Ishas eyum o e e
eh shike kejang eh tohse iykful e e
Jofe kejang ke ngime ndaa
O o kewaih weh beih! Weh chokse ngezhie

Translation:

Who is shouting in the toilet like Tata

Naked.
Go love-making and fell into the toilet
It is proper to make love at home
Oh Oh Tata how you disgrace yourself

Who is shouting in the toilet like Kewaih?

Naked
Go love making and fell into a toilet
It is proper to make love at home
Oh oh Kewaih. how you disgrace yourself.

The Dance

Dancing, says Sorell, is "as old as man and his desire to express himself, to communicate his joys and sorrows, to celebrate and mourn with the most immediate instrument: his body" (9). Dance is a very essential element in the performance of Njange Wan. Except in the context of work, Njange Wan is usually accompanied by dance. As Adejemilua observes:

> Dance is an integral index of human culture, a communicative art and an art of motion which the basic material is the movement of the human body in space and time. Dance is in form of metalanguage and one of the most revealing universal forms of expression by which a lot can be said with the gestures of the arm.(117)

Every member of the Oku society can dance, and most do so from time to time. Participants in Njange Wan range from the infant on his mother's back and the toddler trying a few steps on his own to the wizened adult executing a dance. This dance is not merely a display of physical power and alertness, but an expression of Oku repertoire of knowledge and experiences.

There are two main rhythms for the dancing Njange Wan - the four-beat and six-beat rhythms. With the four beat rhythms, the dancers lift one leg after another, while with the six-beat rhythm, they lift the right leg and stamp the ground

126

with the left leg. The dance is usually begun with the right because the Oku believe that the right is good while the left leg is evil. Hence, when an Oku hits his right leg on an object, he smiles in anticipation of the good fortune that awaits him, but if he hits his left leg, he calls on his ancestors to avert the impending danger. The duration of the dance depends on the length of the song. The dance can either be slow and graceful or fast and forceful. For example, in performance, the women dance with so much force as if to refute the fact that they are now "old and broken":

Kechii kel me nei gwiy ah!
Ah eh eeeee kel wiy siy nai fufe

Kechii kel me nei gwiy ah!
Ah eh eeeee kel wiy siy nai fufe

Ngvuse Kwaake beih ya!
Kel wiy iy nai fufe

Mbiese tongnen eh beih yah!
Kel wiy iy na fufe

Eh nyuke ndumse beih ya!
Kel wiy iy na fufe

Nasse tongnen eh beih yah!
Kel wiy iy na fufe

O ndum wan O
Kel wiy iy nei fufe

O weh ndum ndjumen ah!

Kel wiy iy nei ndjun

Oh dum lome ah!
Kel wiy iy na lom

Kel baba ifum koong sike man ah
Kel wiy ke iy na lom

Oh ndum ndjunmen ah
Kel wiy iy na ndjune

Translation:

On the day I came
Ah eh eede didn't know it will fade

On the day I came
Ah eh e e e e e didn't know it will fade

Fowls cackled in the compound
Didn't know it will fade

Goats bleated in the compound
Didn't know it will fade.

Rat mould was roasted in the compound
Did not know it will fade.

Cows moaned in the compound
Didn't know it will fade.

Oil the child's rat mould
Didn't know it will fade.

Oh rat mould is now old

Didn't know it will hide

Oh Rat mould is now old
Didn't know it will get old

Old dishes
Didn't know it will fade

Sagged breast
Didn't know it will fade...

On the other hand, the dance is slow and graceful in the next song. The women twist their bodies to show how proud and happy they are happy with the arrival of a child.

Wan ah se wan ebo!
Eh loo mom kine - ah?

Maih ah se wan ebo!
Eh loo mom kine ah?
Maih ah se wan wbol, eh loo mom kine - ah?
Babey ya se babey!

Eh loo mom kine - ah?
Nowan ah se Nowan!

Eh loo mom kine ah?
Nowan ah se nowam, eh loo mom kine ah?

Ebliwan ah se ebliwan!
Eh loo mom kine - ah!

Ebliwan ah se ebliwan, eh loo mom kine - ah?
Ndijile ndjileje ndijile ndjileje

Wan ah se wah ebol
Mbofo jo e e

Translation

A child, just a child?
Did this?

Maih a mere child did this?
A father! A real father
Did this?

Maih a mere child did this
A father a real father
Did this?

A father! A real father, did this?
A mother, a true mother?
Did this?

A mother, a true mother? did this?
A sister, a real sister
Did this
A sister, a real sister. did this

Audience: (Interjections)

Though there are stereotype movements performed simultaneously by the dancers, slight individual variations especially in body movements are permitted. Usually, the left arm is relaxed while the right fist is extended forwards. While a soloist sings, the dancers bend very low and regain their standing position as they respond or sing the chorus. As the dancing gains momentum, the dancers as well as the audience begin to chant praises: Iyyole Wan. These are praises: praise names for the child and its lineage, words of appreciation and encouragement to the dancers, or just the ululation of birth.

Some examples are: "chui lu iyzhio e e", "my sun is up" and "the lion of Ndi's family" and "you are more than a leopard". Besides providing and opportunity for the audience to affirm its spiritual identity with the essence of the dance, these interjections increase the tempo of the dance and enhance the mood of the performance.

Performance

The performance of Njange Wan is introduced with the ululation of birth. This sets a hilarious mood. The performance mainly involves sinking and dancing. The length of the performance depends on the mood of both the performers and the audience. As the singing and dancing warm up, more spectators are attracted to the scene. At the climax of the dance, the stamping of feet becomes forceful, and both the performers and the audience chant interjections. At this point there is simultaneous turning by all the performers. The cue to this turning is a clap of the hand by the soloist. The dancers turn clockwise as many times as the soloist wishes. During this performance, the child is brought into the centre of the circle. The baby's mother performs all the actions that the song expects her to perform.

The main structure of the performance of Njange Wan is antiphonal. Here, there are two parties alternating in voicing the lyrics. Most often, there is a soloist calling the tune and the chorus answering. But this is not the rule as there are cases where the two parties are neither distinctively solo nor chorus. The soloist is often an accomplished singer who has the charisma and power to motivate the chorus. She is usually the pivot of the performance. The soloist is not stationed in any strategic position. She is part of the circular formation. This is because there is no permanent soloist and the people believe that the solo and chorus are one. This antiphonal performance creates variety in the performance; the audience is thus not condemned to the drone and monotony of one person. With this form of performance, individuals complement each other so the group dwarfs individual weaknesses. The end of the performance like the beginning is marked by the ululation of birth. Either an incumbent soloist or any of the performers who wishes to start a new song could chant this.

The Performer

The performer is another important clement in the performance of Njange Wan for "oral literature depends on a performer who formulates it in words and there is no other way in which -it can be realised as a literary product" (Finnegan 2). Though any member of Oku society can compose and perform Njange Wan, not everybody that makes the attempt succeeds in producing good songs. Njange Wan is mostly composed by women but the women do not undergo any training and the songs cannot be traced to any particular person.

This anonymity can be explained by the fact that each song has only one existence, that is, when it is sung and the audience knows the singer. As Lord asserts:

> Every poem (flexible forms) bears the signature of its poet/singer. He might have learned the song and the technique of its construction from others but good or bad, the song produced in performance is his own. The audience knows it as his because he is before them (4).

Though the composition of Njange Wan is often impromptu, a lot of selection is done in this process of composing. In an interview with Mama Nurse of Jikejem, a renowned composer of Njange Wan, she has this to say:

> I do not sing everything that comes to my mind. I sort out things and sing those that are pleasing and suit the dance rhythm of Njange Wan. (Interview)

New birth songs must therefore fit into either the four beat or six beat rhythms of Njange Wan. In composing or even singing existing songs, the performers are always conscious of factors controlling the performances. Improvisation plays an important role in the performance because the performer does not produce by what he learned from someone or even composed by himself. He brings the subject matter up to date to make it comprehensible to the contemporary audience. The songs are therefore characterised by continuity, which links the present with the past and variations that spring from the creative forces of the individual. The most distinctive characteristic of Njange Wan is the fluidity of the texts. Each performance is different from another and it is this originality that impresses the audience. There are, however, basic structural patterns at the root of the composition of Njange Wan and the components of such structural patterns are the formula. This is a form of an abstract pattern sentence into which the singer can substitute a great number of words creating a line that will meet the metrical requirement of song. Okpewho defines formula as:

> A basic unit of oral composition from n stock phrase and lines that tradition and long use have stored in the bard's memories, from which he reconstructs fresh ideas and scenes and thus supports the overall fabric of history. (138)

The composers do not just compose anything. They use the formula to compose so their songs are easily identified as Njange Wan. For example, it is mandatory that new songs fit into the dance rhythm of Njange Wan. The epithet is one of the formulas used in Njange Wan. These are phrases, which serve as a means of description of an incident, person or themes. Some examples are a "cutlass hand" and "The lion of Ndi's family" and "you are more than a leopard". Since the audience is not captive and will not listen to pure didacticism however instructive, the success of the performance of Njange Wan depends on the performer's ability to stimulate enthusiasm in the audience. The performers thus supplement their efforts with dramatic actions, gestures, charming voices, facial expressions, mimicry and dancing. The performance of all the songs in this collection is accompanied by dramatisation.

Our critical objective is to find out how the Oku people appreciate and appraise their birth songs, how the performance of birth songs affects the audience as well as how the audience's reaction and criticism influence the quality of the performance. This is because it is our contention that we cannot fully understand and appreciate the birth songs of the Oku if we do not know either how they appreciate and criticise them. As Arewa and Dundes maintain:

> If there is oral literature, there is oral literary criticism. The shelves of folklore are filled with text and material telling us what folklore means and what its value is, but few of these explanations and evaluations comes from the folk. Native literary criticism, which could be considered as an aspect of "ethno-literature" does not eliminate the need for analytical literary criticism, but it certainly should be recorded as part of the ethnographic context of folklore, both for its own interest and because native interpretation of folklore, influence the decision to employ a particular one in particular situation. (38)

Similarly, R.D. Abraham reminds folklorists to always endeavour in their investigations to find out how the performance of any item of folklore by the folks affects the audience to remember that:

> in analyzing traditional expressive literature our method should emphasising all aspects of the aesthetic performance: performance items and audience participation, this method will brins to&cthcr the

demands of the functionalist school of anthropologist, who see folklore in its contextual frame, and of the formalistic perception of recent literary criticism. (144)

Although Njange Wan could be performed without an audience, the informants interviewed insist on the need for an audience for an effective performance. Amali divides the audience of oral literature into "the immediate and remote audience" (11-12). In Njange Wan, the immediate audience are those physically present but who participate in the performance with their sense of hearing psychologically and emotionally. The audience is unrestricted and varied. Some come to watch the performance out of curiosity and love for the songs. Others are familiar with the music and want to listen to the creative variations that may come in the course of the extant performance. Some attend to grace the occasion and give moral support to the performer. Others attend because they are leaders of the community and have certain functions to perform during the celebration.

The attitude expected of the audience is not one restrained, contemplative behaviour as is the case with some typically western audience, but one of dramatic expressions of feeling. Njange Wan audience is a force to reckon with because

> the presence and participation of the audience influences the animation of the performance, the spontaneous selection of music, the range textual improvisation and other details and this
> stimulus to creative activity is welcomed and even sought by the performer (Nketia 33)

136

The performers count themselves lucky if they gain the empathy and co-operation of their audience. The audience shows its appreciation of the performance by joining in the dance, singing the refrain, or praising the performers through interjections. These interjections enliven the performance and mark the climax. The reaction of the audience is a barometer with which the performer judges her performance in Njange Wan. A melodious voice is one of the criteria for judging a performer. She is expected to vocalise the words of the song clearly and distinctly. The audience also ensures that new songs fit into the rhythm of Njange Wan. This is because the audience and the performer are one and as Sekoni opines "they are not only concerned with the examination of the dominant values of their community but also interested in the encapsulation of such discourse in an aesthetic form" (1990: 142). When a song is well sung, everyone admires it; when it is badly sung everybody knows it. Though no singer is applauded for a brutal violation of the essential legacy, what Lord calls "the historic truth of traditional song" (28) the performers of Njange Wan are not completely bound to culture, for as Okpewho states "the aesthetic principle in oral arts involves a slight tilt of the balance in favour of beauty over truth" (25). If the language and content are fresh, the performer is praised for her creativity and imagination.

While discussing this relationship between culture and performance, Bennet remarks that:

> Both an audience's reactions to a text or performance and the text itself are bound within cultural limits. Yet as diachronic analysis makes apparent, those limits are continually tested and invariably broken. Culture cannot be held as a fixed entity, as a set of constant

rules, but instead it must be seen as in a position of inevitable flux. (101)

Besides performing songs which arc realistic, the performer is expected to be unique, to improvise on the existing formula to reformulate the traditional subject to bring it up to date and make it palatable and understandable to the contemporary audience. It is evident form our discussion of the role of the audience that the Oku use four parameters to distinguish between a good and bad song. These are authenticity, clarity, functionality and originality. When a song is badly sung, the audience could either hiss or leave the arena of the performance.

Chapter 8

Riddles and Bash

C. Ce

LITTLE has been written about the riddle genre of Africa's oral art apart from scattered references in some research efforts by western scholars. Yet the riddles of African oral literature still survive as a literary genre in its own right with short diction and imposed meanings, stock devices and stock answers repeated almost word for word in communities where they flourish.

Among the children of Alaa[1] the value of the riddle and bash contests is not just in the educational or entertainment motif. There lies some superabundant wit in the prolific deployment of imagery, epithets and symbolism from the repertoire of Alaa tradition and culture. Alaa's progeny themselves are regular contestants and have, over time, cultivated so much artistry in this artistic form that they must generally come to be recognised as bards in their own right.

The creative genius in African literary tradition is often indebted to his immediate environment or larger society. It is the society that provides him with linguistic and literary traditions in terms of a common language or dialect, metaphor, imagery, and proverbs. But this in no way dims the creative vision that drives the spirit of his art and the genuineness of his work.

'Genius' here implies the artiste's ability to effect some variations on this body of existing traditional sources at his disposal. 'Some traditions allow for considerable individualistic expression,' says Abdulkadir. '(So) the poet must however rely to some extent on traditional forms and structures... and traditional materials in (his)... composition. (Abalagu, et al) Thus the evidence of performance reveals that it is the personal dynamics that must coalesce acceptably with the artiste's traditional repertoire in order to make the final piece a unique and aesthetically pleasing experience.

This is what makes the elaborate riddle contests of Alaa a richer concatenation of expressions of intrinsic poetic value than ordinary riddles and one can agree no less with Jack Mapanje that 'the person who can complete the metaphor (and symbols laden in this art genre)... is well equipped to understand (great) poetry.' (83))

No riddle was ever established by any particular individual. African riddles rise with communal linguistic heritage and take their place among the idioms, proverbs and poetic expressions of the people. The great don John himself once said of the riddle and bash contests during his own time:

> after the farming season when children had little to do, this contest was there to keep them busy, or when they grow rather restless they are called together and riddles are thrown to them. (Interviews)

140

If those games were consequently borne out of the educational need of the community -the need to educate the children and improve their sense of observation of lives around them, contemporary social events take their place as sources of innovations. For example, a drunkard, a habitually late cook, a scandal or legal tussle would easily form a most entertaining allusion-laden bash.

Creative Riddle and Bash Action in Alaa

Agreeably with Hagler, 'performance is a doing art' (81), and 'an overt behaviour as a realisation of an underlying knowledge on the part of the speaker.' (Hymes 186) For Alaa's children, knowledge implies the traditional wisdom to interpret and recreate riddles, realised by elaborate dramatic enactment. Earlier, this was usually performed among age-grades during the moonlit frolics. De Joe of Okpula,[2] explains this enactment in detail:

> One age-grade would sit in a corner, split into two groups. Each group sits in one line, side by side, and facing the other group similarly organised. Now one member fires the first shot at his counterpart. If the answer proffered is correct, it's one point for the side, otherwise it is one point against the side. At the end of it all, are records are reviewed to determine the winner, (Interviews)

The bash is organised in a similar way usually involving boys on the one side and girls on the other.

> Girls stand in a row, facing the boys who swagger defiantly before them. This usually marks the end of

the session. The bash begins when one of the boys makes some rude advances to a female counterpart, and she retorts with an abuse. The other boys remonstrate sharply and a battle of wits begins. It usually ends with all returning to their homes, claiming victory over their opponents, (Interviews)

Nowadays however, moonlight plays and dances have virtually disappeared from most African villages. But this is in no way a limitation to their enjoyment of an art that has become a way of life for the people of Alaa. Public performances are more spontaneous. Two youths engage themselves in the riddle context and take notes to determine the winner where there is no audience.[4] However, the presence of an audience enlivens the bash performance more. Here is a typical occasion of bash performance: A cluster of small groups in a public tap. There are few adults, a number of young people with an admixture of male and female sexes. There are less conscious polarities of participants into opposing camps, in other words, a free-for-all session. So members of the audience are participants at the same time. Typically, a player finds his supporters among those who mock his opponent. Quite dramatically, one supporter might turn around to be an antagonist, pitching his tent with the group that is fast gaining the louder ovation. This *volte face* adds boisterous laughter to the game.

Challenger (1):
Chidi
Maka mkpuru rice
Ka iji gbaa nna gi
Ekpuruke n'ahia ukwu taa

Translation:

142

For one grain of rice, Chidi,
You threw your father
In wrestling match today.

(Chidi's reply)
Ohoo?
Maka ibe akidi Otu-ibe akidi
Igbara nne gi N'ala

Really?
But you for half a been-seed
wrestled your mother
to the ground.

At this point, Uka, another participant wades in, pitching his tent with Chidi. This audience-narrator interaction provides a common spur for the creative ingenuity of the youths. It is now a free-for-all entertainment spree of verbal bashing and mockery.

Uka:
Eze mhuru gi n'onu
Dika foku ekwensu
Ji-ata ugba

Challenger (1):
Iya!
Obu ya kpatara
Iji eme onu
Ka ina-ami
Ndi opo avu.

Ma nti gi-a
Buchaa otua

Dika afo ime onwa asaa

Translation:

Uka:
The teeth in your mouth
Are like the roasting prongs
of the devil.

Challenger (1):
Oh yeah? Is that why
Your mouth looks
Like you had kiss
Of a leper's sores.

Now see, see
how your chin is bulging
Like a seven-month pregnancy.

A clever performance wins a loud complimentary remark 'heee!' a dull one meets with a universal 'kooo!' which confirms the assumption that for the performers 'their greatest appeal lies in their lively spontaneity and the performer's unquestioned familiarity with the traditional element of his art. (de Graft 170)

Challenger:

Ugbua kedu onye
Onu ya na-esi
Dika ogwe N'ejula eju.

Now who is it
That his mouth reeks
Like a latrine

144

That's filled up.

Ma ahu mhuru
Gbara okporo iji
Anya gharii.

You farted on the street
And even the flies
Went rigid with fright

Lee ka ukwu
Na-ahu gi ririri
Dika oche ndi A
nu odogwo.

But why does your leg
Shake so badly (ririri)
Like the rickety table Of
stale-meat butchers.

Dada, isi gi
Eyika nke udele
Mmiri mara.

Dada, your hair
Reminds me of a vulture
Soaked in the rain.

Obu ya mere
Iji dowe onu
Ka mkpi na-esi
Mamiri ya.

So that is why Your nose
is hung At that angle
like a he-goat on heat?

he

The test of creative wit is that one does not lack the verbal dart to throw at his opponent in this admix of imaginative improvisations. Even when core traditional imagery is exhausted, participants begin to improvise with contemporary incidents in the community. Such individual artistry differs among the youths, and it is this peculiar attribute in each of the participants that informs their different 'techniques of ornamentation.'(Abdulkadir, 1980)

> Ezilam ukwu gi
> Ukwu ndanda gi
> Agaghi ekoli nke
> Dee Mathias

> Now you do not need
> To swing your hips to me
> That ant-waist of yours
> Cannot rouse old
> De Mathias....

These techniques are prolific in riddles more so as the 'battle' itself is a spontaneous activity, demanding fast thinking. But behind all the continuum of spontaneity and innovation, traditional texts abound from the overflow of exuberant creative genius. In fact these young adults start from the familiar traditional sources to their own improvisations with exercise of their wide imaginative powers, aimed of course, at outwitting one another. This is because 'traditional African life in general is rich in poetic expressions... in a sense that is far reaching, for they are not only spontaneous and realistic but also beautiful.' (Egudu 79) One is correct to add that it is the spontaneity of its reaction that marks the beauty and liveliness of most riddle performances.

Patterns of Associations

A discernible literary trait in the art of riddle performance is the pattern of association of images, objects and life. Parry's formulaic theory sees the formula as a group of words regularly employed under the same metric conditions to express a given essential idea. (Abdulkadir 80) This definition is implicit to the 'metric condition' of traditional songs or musical renditions. However, the formulaic theory of Parry is not only employed in terms of the 'metric conditions' but the epithet-formula, the noun-formula and verb-formula could also be employed, not in relation to the metrical condition but for what Chukwuma Azuonye calls the 'semantic factor.' According to Azuonye, traditional epithet is not used for any metrical convenience... the use of formulas, especially epithet formula...is governed by the semantic factor of association rather than any of the mechanical metre.[5]

The latter's position is made more plausible with the traditional core epithets, symbolism and imagery from which the youthful bards of Alaa draw their sources adding their own individual talents and enhancing the process of creativity in a pattern distinctive of riddle and bash art. These patterns complement the formulas -usually transferred epithets combined with traditional symbolism in the course of performance. For example, 'ose' (pepper) 'oyogho' (plantain) and 'akummo' (coconut) are symbols of multiple blessings. The little pods of pepper on the plant, the heavy coconut pods and the cluster of plantains, are symbols of procreation and multiplicity.

In the same vein, their manner of presentation in the riddle is laden with transferred epithets, for example,

> Tell me who
> is the rich housewife
> with many many children?
> (Answer: The Pepper.)

> Tell me the torch
> that makes
> the whole world warm

> The seasonal guest
> Of all the world
> (The Moon)

The coconut tree and the plantain acquire a peculiar character of aloof sequestration from all activity.

> Tell me who
> Is that queer woman
> That keeps her children
> In the heavens

> Answer: Plantain

> Tell me who
> Is the foolish maid
> that breast-feeds children
> over the rafters

> Answer: Coconut.

The association of 'breast-feeding' with the coconut differentiates if from the plantain, although both (plantain and coconut) share similar conditions of high sequestration. Ripe paw-paw fruits are represented as,

> The fair bride who
> must not touch the mat
> (for her husband).

Just as the image of breast-feeding links the coconut with the riddle, so does the association of the fair bride 'who cannot touch the mat for her husband,' traditionally indicate the ripe papaw that must not be allowed to fall on the dry ground from the tree. We equally see the sense of symbolic representations in the moon. The moon in riddles indicates inexhaustible universality, and infinity. In riddles there are ways in which the epithet formula of a yam slice, or fire, could be used to describe the moon, for example,

> The slice of yam
> That feeds the world.

The sun on the other hand is alluded as the firewood.

> the firewood that burns
> world without end.

Acoustics and Improvisations

Some sounds in the riddle occupy a distinct traditional acoustic device used in representing particularly related phenomenon; for example, the sound 'kpam' is an acoustic formula that is usually employed for the breaking of wood. Other acoustic device like the sound 'kpum' depict the sound of metal on wood. Generally, the acoustics of Alaa's riddles are rarely manipulated differently otherwise the meaning is lost.

Thus, the sound,

> *kon ti*
> *kon kon kon ti.*

> (Crack not kernels
> Near the pit.)

is usually recited along with the tonal recitation, in order that the meaning i.e., the verbal translation mimics fairly the sound, 'kon ti' which in itself is an allophone for the cracking of shells.

Similarly, 'tum tum, gem gem' is an acoustic device for the quick, lithe movements of rodents. In riddles it is the traditional Alaa onomatopoeia for the smart quick prance of the squirrel. In totality the acoustic formula of 'kpum' (for cutting), 'kon ti' (for cracking), 'turn turn' (for quickness), 'kpam' (for breaking) form part of the source repertoire of the riddles.

Imagery of Bash Contests

During the bash session of this literary fair, a range of traditional core images arc deployed in performance. Alaa youths are mostly informed by their early or original knowledge of the traditional similes and metaphors acquired from many series of performances. The allusions are generally ludicrous, highly exaggerated but suggestive of underlying meanings, for example,

For one grain of rice

> Nathan wrested the throne
> from his own father

This abuse has a dramatic effect by its suggestion of greed and avarice, which is even aggravated by a more ludicrous 'offence,'

> And, for one half been seed
> You, Ekwedike,
> You wrestled your mother
> At the market square.

The latter counter fire profanes the traditional respect for womanhood while rice grain and bean seed are symbols of foreign taste. In a larger perspective, it means superseding imported values (rice and beans) over our own tradition (of reverence for father and mother). The implication of greed is seen in the very mean proportion of the foreign diet - 'grain of rice' and 'half a bean seed.'
Furthermore the depiction of Ike's mouth that

> ...reeks
> like the pit latrine
> very nearly full...

> or

> a fart...
> that shocked the fly dumb-

are metaphors of unpleasant health conditions or poor hygiene. The motif of ugliness is usually presented in these images that always recur in the bash:

old vulture
Soaked in the rain

chin
like the bulge
of Maria's belly

teeth
the roasting fork of the devil.

These, in their varied manners of presentation, are portraits of physical incongruity, Elements of Christian myths (fork of the devil) are sprinkled freely. They are allusions that the children have come to learn in the course of their religious exposures and they are drawn from the traditional repertoire which the people use to satirise the physical attributes and mannerisms of their opponents.

Antiphonal wit of Riddles and Bash

The pattern of riddle call and the response is a traditional stock-opening device always observed in the recitations. The challenger rises to the initiative by calling the name of his chosen opponent. The opponent who then accepts the challenge replies 'Ehee!' along with the audience, who all anticipate the first 'attack.' It is an original device which is used to prepare the participants for the questions and abuses involved in the contest. Every participant begins in this way until the excitement gathers momentum, and the stock call-response is abandoned briefly. This especially occurs in the bash. Riddle poetry, through the years, has been greatly enriched by performers'

152

excited contests. By their sheer power of imagination, and in their vociferous excitement, they display artistry and ingenuity, by exploring the original traditional patterns or formula, 'they also capitalise on incidents, recreating, refurbishing and enhancing their oral heritage. In this stock formula of opening call and response, ingenious children bring their talents to play. Deliberate prolongation of call is an art that achieves some dramatic Here, for example, Chidi not just takes on his opponent, but also invites the audience.

Chidi: Turum ya nu Saa

All: Saa!

Chidi: Tuorum ya nu Saa

All: Saa!

Chidi: Tuorum ya nu Saa

All: Saa! Saa! Saa!

Chidi:
All hail him 'Sir!'

All: Sir!

Chidi: All hail him 'Sir'.'

All: Sir! Sir! Sir!

This deliberate rolling and prolongation of the call might be accompanied by a dramatic battle-cry. The intention may be to create some comic effect that eventually wears down the other side and throws them off their guard when the shot is suddenly released. In some instances the stock call may be intoned in a familiar lyric which enhances the dramatic nature of the contest. Gesticulations might feature prominently, apart from the mock dance and battle-cry. A conscious attempt by a riddle participant might be made to dramatise,

> what else that clapped
> 'kpam' into the bush.

As a cue the exclamation of 'kpam' is followed by a clap. In the bash session, the 'ant-waist' or the nose that looks like that of the billy goat, the flatulent chin, could be acted out in a way that would enhance or aggravate the ugliness of the physical attribute. Of course these effects are easily achieved by ingenious ones who have the peculiar ability to twist some parts of their bodies to achieve desired effect.

Poetics of Alaa Riddles

From observations, the (riddle) is an elevated poetic game that demands hard mental exercise with its transferred epithets and symbolism. Since these riddles involve the teachings imparted by parents, both players and audience operate from a common source so the repertoire of traditional epithets and allusions are familiar.

(Call)

gwam nne umu hiri
ahu gburu gburu

(Response) Ose.

Gwam nwa bu nna ya uzo –
bu nna ya uzo
Taa Oji oha
(Response) Anya

Gwam okoro chara nzu-
 okoro chara nzu
Baa n'ohia
(Response) Okpo Ugu.

Tell me who
is the mother with children
round and round her side
Pepper (answer)

Tell me who
is the son that took the cola
before his father did.
Eye (answer)

Tell me who
the young man in the bush
all white with chalk
Fluted Pumpkin (answer).

This group has thrown three darts. It is the turn of the
other opposing camp.

Gwam agbogho iru

Mmanu mmanu.
(Response) Okwuruegbe.

Gwam nwanyi kpo umu
Rigoo n'elu.
(Response) Oyogho.

Gwam otu ibe ji
Zuru oha afo
(Response) Onwa

Tell me
who is the young girl
with the fairest of faces
(Response) The Paw-paw

Woman with her children
hung up in the skies
(*Response*) The Plantain

The slice of yam
that feeds the world.
(Response) the Moon

The questions come in quick succession. If the answer given is incorrect the audience and participants may offer a loud correction. There is equally the riddle of sounds and their meanings, similar to what Finnegan calls 'acoustic analogy.' This is the ability of the participants to interpret the sounds and rhythms of unnamed objects or events. They are mainly tonal riddles '...in which there is a kind of rhythm in the syllables so that the questions are like two little verses balancing each other in a particular way.' (Finnegan, 1970) They provide poetic lyricism to riddles, for example,

Gwam, kon ti
Kon kon ti.

Answer: Crack not kernels
Near a pit (latrine)

The tonal rendition is done in such a way that it fairly corresponds to the verbal version.

Gwam
ereghe re - ti rere
Answer: anaghi agba ose na-anya.

(Do not rub)
Pepper in the eyes)

Some of these tonal riddles are also ideophonic expressions of given objects.

Gwam kpom ti
Kpo.

(Response) Ikwe n'odu
(Mortar and Pestle)

Gwam kpum
Yoooo.

(Response) -aka nkwu
The (falling) Palm frond.

Some are onomatopoeia that represent traditionally recognised sound effects.

Gwam ihe gbara 'kpam!'

Baa n'ohia
(Answer) ugba.

What made a noise ('kpam')
And ran into bush
(Oil bean seed)

Gwam tum tum
Gem gem.

(Response)
Oso mgbada bu n'ugwu.
(The hare race is fastest on a hill)

Other cases of modification of composition abound. The universe of moon, stars and firelight has been manipulated in a similar stylistic manner:

Gwam
Mpalaka
Zuru uwa nile

Onye ije
Nleta uwa

These are the ingenious improvisations that have been employed from the universal attributes of the moon. In the following presentation, the 'smart eye' in the riddle form, is modified from the well-known son that took the kola offering before his father to a brazen

(the) clever man
who first slept with his
own brother's wife....
or the

wily man who
seduces a wife before
her husband

This variation still retains the formulaic symbolism of
'the clever man'   which 'the eye' traditionally occupies
in a riddle. Such variations frequently occur and are
usually incorporated into the body of traditional texts.
Ingenious performers would cultivate historical incidents
into riddles:

Okpo nkita Eje ikpe
(Mbama)

(He taketh a dog
To a law suit)
Mbama (answer)

In this dart, Mbama, a man with the notoriety of
frequent police cases, becomes the answer. The essential
device is the satirisation of the eccentric who sees fit to
take his dog to a lawsuit. There are further examples of
local satires through the riddle art form:

Gwam
Okwa nka
Igbeogologo

Translation:
Tell me
Who is the carpenter
Of long boxes
Answer: de Mike.

The (exaggeration) epithet of the carpenter is part of the comic sense of humour of some Alaa's exuberant youths. Some allophones have been created out of past incidents of comic nature. The following satiric verse, for example, is a satire of two bed mates.

Gwam
'Piakam
Piaaa!'
(Answer:
'Theresa and John
are on bed')

There are instances where riddles had emanated from some proverbs commonly used among the elderly members of the lineage. Here the clever children turn these special proverbs and idioms into some kind of evocation. For example, this riddle,

Kedu
Ahu anyuru n'elu
Mere anu gwungem

Translation:
what
is the fart from above
that stunned the bee

obviously comes from the traditional proverb that states that a proverb said to a woman is like fart from a tree top (which no one can guess the direction it came of proverbs would reveal such types drawn from imagistic, as against linguistic, parallels. These often combine to form derivations for the riddle genre particularly when they come as extractions from familiar proverbs of the community:

Linguistic type:

'A proverb said to a woman is like a fart from the tree top which no-one could guess the direction it came.'

Riddle:

gwam
sihu anyuru n'elu
mere anu gwungem

Translation:
the wine tapper's fart
that puzzles the bees.
(Answer: A proverb)

The above exemplifies some clever versification and allophonisation of the proverb. The riddle comes from the traditional activity of wine tapping and bees. Bees here represent the woman who, from the traditional point of view, is not capable of comprehending the 'profundity' of proverbs (even though some women are better at the art of proverbs than their male counterparts). In tills way the long proverb itself has been adapted from its linguistic parallel to a rather 'compressed' or 'imagistic' poetry.

A further example could be drawn from these proverb and riddle.

Proverb:

Anwu ehihie adighi egbu agwo

(The twilight is not enough for the snake to bask in.)

Riddle:
>   gwam
>   Oku na-enwu adighi achu agwo

>   what
>   is the fire
>   the snake doesn't fear
>   Twilight (answer).

Both samples trace the influence of proverbs in some riddles of the people. Ruth Finnegan was therefore correct in her observation that '...among some peoples, riddles may be particularly closely connected with proverbs so that either the answer or even both parts of the riddle are sayings accepted in other contexts as proverbs.' (1970) However, the difference between proverbs and riddles lies in the poetry of the latter, the personification of the inanimate, accordance of anthropomorphic personality to animal species and deployment of deeper levels of meaning (allusions) to otherwise simple ideas drawn from the general flora and fauna of the community.

All in all, the creative wit of oral riddles and bash forms, like oral literature in Africa, is a continually expanding and enhancing totality, with lots of opportunity for variations eloquence, dramatic devices and all the individual artistry which go with the performance of this most intriguing art. No wonder then that it is so deservedly prized among the people of Alaa till date.

Notes and Bibliography

Chapter One
Oratorical Strategies in African Literature

Notes

1.Tala, K.I. An Introduction to Cameroon Oral Literature, The University of Yaounde, 1984, p.64.

2.Audu Bature, Labarin Sarkin Tsuntsaye, A collection of Unpublished Haussa Tales, Garoua, 1989.

3.Tale narrated to author by Nhon Ekukwe Sumelong of Nkikoh village, Bangem on 23 May 2003.

4.Excerpts taken from an issue of "Afrique Etats Unis", a publication of the American Cultural Centre, Yaounde.

Works Cited

Camara, Laye. *The Dark Child*. Trans. James Kirkup & Ernest Jones. New York: The Noonday Press, 1994.

Ce, Chin. *Children of Koloko*. Morrisville: Lulu. 2000.

Courlander, Harold. *A Treasury of African Folklore*. New York: Crown Publishers Inc. 1975.

Current Concerns. "The Dark Child: The Autobiography of an African Boy by Camara Laye." Current Concerns 4 (2004) <www.currentconcerns.ch/archive/2004/04 /20040414.php>.

Grants, Amanda. "Memory, Transition and Dialogue: The Cyclic Order of Chin Ce's Oeuvres." *Journal of African Literature and Culture*. IRCALC: 2006. 11-29.

Okolie, Maxwell. "Childhood in African Literature: A Literary Perspective." *Childhood in African Literature*. Eds. Eldred Durosimi Jones & Marjorie Jones. Oxford: James Currey Ltd., 1998. 29-35.

Chapter Two
Oral Rhythms of Achebe's Fiction

Notes

1.See Abdul Mohammed, 'Sophisticated Primitivism: The Syncretism of Oral and Literate Modes in Achebe's Things Fall Apart, Ariel, 15, 4 (1984), pp. 19-39.

2.Gareth Griffiths, 'Language and Action in the Novel of Chinua Achebe, African Literature Today Vol 5, (1971), p.89.

3.See Emmanuel Obiechina, Culture, Tradition and Society in the West African Novel, Cambridge: Cambridge University Press, 1975, repr. 1980, p.27.

4.Isidore Okpewho, 'The Epic in Africa: Towards a Poetics of the Oral Performance,' New York: Columbia University Press, 1979, p. 72.,

5.Stith Thompson, ed. Four Symposia on Folklore, Bloomington; Indiana University press, 1953, p. 308.

6.Chinua Achebe, Things Fall Apart, London: Heinemann, repr. 1982. All references arc to this edition and are cited in. the text.

7.See John S. Mbiti, African Religion and Philosophy, London: Heinemann, 1970, p. 19 Mbiti says, 'when Africans reckon time, it is for a concrete and specific purpose in connection with events but not just for the sake of mathematics.'

8.Chinua Achebe, Arrow of God, London,: Heinemann, revised edition, 1982. All references are to this edition and arc cited in the text.

9.Mbiti, loc. cit., 'The day, the month, the year, one's life time or human history are all divided up or reckoned according to their specific events or it is these that makes them meaningful.'

10.Ibid., p. 2ll. Mbiti attests that this basic concept of time underlies the life of those who live not only in the villages but also to a great extent those who work or live in the cities.

11.Chinua Achebe A Man of the People, London: Heinemann, repr. 1982. All references are to this edition and are cited in the text.

12.Majorie Winters, 'An Objective Approach to Achebe's Style'

14.Research in African Literatures, 12,1 (Spring 1981), p. 62.

15.Ruth Finnegan, Oral Poetry: Its Nature, Significance; Social Context, London: Cambridge University Press, 1977, p.129.

16.Okpewho, op. cit, p. 194.

17.Chinua Achebe, No Longer At Ease, London: Heinemann, repr. 1981. All references arc to this edition and arc cited in the text.

19.Winters, op. cit, p.62.

Chapter Three
Relearning the Song that Truly Speaks

Notes

1.All translations pertaining to this collection and other Couto's writings/titles are my own.

2.This paper is based on some of the ideas discussed in my doctoral thesis, in which I explore with greater detail some of the intersections between Western psychoanalysis, Jungian psychology, écriture féminine, Lévinasian, Irigaraian and Heideggerian philosophy, Buddhism and African epistemologies (using as basis the works of four world writers).

3.Rothwell further argues that Couto's project of endogeniation is particularly clear in his recent novel O Último Voo do Flamingo ('The Last Flight of the Flamingo'). See A Postmodern Nationalist, specifically section 7: "Finding the Nation's Phallus: Expelling the UN Specter from Mozambique" 158-169 and "Conclusion" 170-2.

4.See for example, A varanda do frangipani ('Under the Frangipani') Cada homen é uma raça ('Every Man is a Race'), Estórias abensonhadas ('Blissfully Dreamed Stories') and Terra sonâmbula ('Sleepy Land').

5.Couto's introductory quotation seems to associate the sun with the masculine, the rational, the compartmentalized and violent forces, and the moon with the feminine, the earth, the tender and the holistic.

6.For further discussions of the concepts of "dead talk" and "overstanding" see also Velma Pollard's book Dread Talk: The Language of Rastafarians and J. Edward Chamberlin's Come Back to Me My Language.

7.See "Freud and Love: Treatment and its Discontents" 240-248 in The Kristeva Reader and Pouvoirs de l'horreur 9-24.

8.The reason why the song-language of the little girl is able to reach the subconscious of the father: music (like poetry) functions as the pre-symbolic language or way of communicating, which has the power to liberate us from societal (conscious) constraints and allows us to go deeper inwards.

9.As Lewis Hyde puts it, "The trickster is a boundary-crosser," the one who blurs distinctions and connections between "right and wrong, sacred and profane, clean and dirty, male and female, young and old, living and dead (7)."

10.In Portuguese, when someone is angry or acts/reacts in an unpredictable way, we often say that the person "está de lua" (literally meaning 'is with moon') or "está enluarado" ('is moony') or "está com a lua" ('is with the moon'). All of these expressions imply that that the person is mad and has lost the ability to reason properly (he/she is a lunatic).

11.Couto is a language relativist like Ngũgĩ (see Decolonizing the Mind) or Whorf (see Language, Thought, and Reality) and others. Language relativists believe language molds the way humans see reality and themselves. Different languages emerge out of different socio-cultural, physical, ontological and epistemological environments and thus no language will 'say' the same thing. By creating new words, Couto is writing in a 'new' Portuguese –just like many other postcolonial writers who write in 'new' englishes in order to try and recapture a more 'authentic' post-colonial subject, a subject that is more faithful to the pre-colonial ways of being an 'seeing'.

12.See "Chief Characteristics of Satori" in The Essentials of Zen Buddhism 163-168 and The Quest for Self 119.

13.In A Postcolonial Nationalist Rothwell also discusses the importance and constant presence of water in Couto's writings and its frequent association with the unconscious realm, the realm that allows one to have access to dream and imagination and thus 'encounter' all possibilities (see "Seaing into the Unconscious: The Role of Water in Mia Couto" 91-132).

Works Cited

Chamberlin, J. Edward. *Come Back to me My Language: Poetry and the West Indies*. Urbana: University of Illinois P, 1993.

– – –. *If This is Your Land, Where Are Your Stories?: Finding Common Ground*. Toronto: Alfred A. Knopf Canada, 2003.

Couto, Mia. *A varanda do frangipani: romance*. Lisboa: Editorial Caminho, 1996.

– – –. *Cada homen é uma raça: estórias*. Lisboa: Editorial Caminho, 1990.

– – –. *Estórias abensonhadas: contos*. Lisboa: Editorial Caminho, 1994.

– – –. *Contos do Nascer da Terra*. Lisboa: Editorial Caminho, 1997.

– – –. *Terra sonâmbula: romance*. Lisboa: Editorial Caminho, 1992.

Hyde, Lewis. *Trickster Makes This World: Mischief, Myth, And Art*. New York: Farrar, Straus and Giroux, 1998.

Iisuka, Takeshi. *The Quest for the Self: Zen in Business and Life*. New York and London: 1995.

Jeremias, Luísa. "O meu segredo é transportar a meninice." *A Capital*. Lisboa, 8 de Dezembro de 2000. 29 April 2002 <http://www.instituto-camoes.pt/arquivos/literatura/ mcoutoentrv.htm>.

Ki-Zerbo, Joseph, ed. *General History of Africa, Vol. I: Methodology and African Prehistory*. London: Heinemann, 1989.

Kristeva, Julia. *Pouvoirs de l'horreur: essai sur l'abjection*. Paris: Éditions du Seuil, 1980.

– – –. *The Kristeva Reader.* Ed. Moi Toril. New York: Columbia UP, 1986.

Ngũgĩ, wa Thiong'o. *Decolonizing the Mind: The Politics of Language in African Literature.* London: Currey, 1986.

Plato. *Timaeus and Critias.* Trans. and Intro Desmond Lee. London: Penguin Books, 1977.

Pollard, Velma. *Dread Talk: The Language of Rastafari.* Kingston, Jamaica: Canoe P, 1994.

Rothwell, Phillip. *A Postmodern Nationalist: Truth, Orality, and Gender in the Work of Mia Couto.* Lewisburg: Bucknell University Press, 2004.

Suzuki, Daisetz Teitaro. *The Essentials of Zen Buddhism: Selected from the Writings of Daisetz* T. Suzuki. Ed. and Intro. Bernard Phillips. Westport, Conn.: Greenwood Press, 1973.

Walcott, Derek. *Collected Poems,* 1948-1984. New York: Farrar, Straus and Giroux, 1986.

Whorf, Benjamin. *Language, Thought, and Reality: Selected Writings.* Cambridge: M.I.T. P, 1964.

Chapter Four
Comparing the Child Hero

Notes

1.This book is actually published in French, under the title; Chinua Achebe et la tragedies de I' Histoire. The English version, both of the title and the quotations from the book, are own translation.

2.Le Pain des Reves, (Bread of the Imagination) (1942), a semi autobiographical novel, was like a bridge which the author (Louis Guilloux) built between the horror of 1942 France and his childhood in Brittany during Second World War. Guilloux was born in Saint-Brieue in 1899 and died in 1980.

Works Cited

Melone, Thomas. *Chinua Achebe et la Tragedie de I'Histoire*. Paris, Presence Africaine, 1973, pp. 12,77, 149.

Ngugi Wa Thiong'o. *Weep not, child*. Heinemann, 1962.

Ferdinand, Oyono. *Houseboy*. London: Heinemann 1966. (First published in Paris, under the title *Une vie de boy,* Editions Julliard, 1956.

Robert, Marthe. *Roman des Origenes*. Origenes du Roman, Paris, Gallimard, Tel, 1972.

Chapter Five
Hearts and Ballads

Works Cited

Acholonu, Catherine. *Nigeria in the Year 1999*. Owerri: Town Publishers, 1985

Haring, Bernard. *Free and Faithful in Christ: Moral Theology for Priests and Laity*. Middlegreen: Slough: St. Paul's Publications, 1981. Vol. II.

Madiebo, Alexander. *The Nigerian Revolution and the Biafran War* Enugu: Fourth Dimension Publishers, 1980.

Odumegwu-Ojukwu, Emeka. *Because I am Involved*. Ibadan: Spectrum Books Ltd. 1989.

Ofeimun, Odia. *The Poet Lied*. London: Longman Drumbeat, 1980.

Osundare, Niyi. Songs of the Market Place Ibadan: New Horn Press, 1983.

Ugah, Ada. *Naked Hearts*. Braunton, Devonshire: MerlinBooks Ltd, 1983.

.... *The Ballads of the Unknown Soldier*. Enugu: Harris Publishers Ltd. 1989.

Chapter Six
Njange Wan

Works Cited

Abrahams, R.D. "Introductory Remarks to a Theory of Folklore," *Journal of American Folklore. 81 (1988)* 144-145

Adejemllua, M. Segun. "The Artistic Process, Myth; and Choreographic Patterns in Yoruba Dance Form: An Introductory Survey." *Contemporary Issues in African Arts.* eds. Uka, G. and Segun, A.M. Nigeria; Femi-Sola Print (1994). 117-124.

Amali, O. O. S. "Evaluation of J. P. Clark's Research Method used in "The Ozidi Saga." A paper presented in Ahmadu Bello University (March, 21 1981) 11-12.

Arewa, E.O. and Alan Dundes, "Proverbs and the Ethnography of Speaking Folklore." *Analytical Essays in Folklore.* New York: Mouton Publishers 1975 252 - 333'

Ben-Amos, Dan. "Analytical Categories and Ethnic Genres." Folklore Genre, ed. Dan ben-Routledge, 1990.

Coffin, T.P. and K. Cohening. eds. *Folklore in America.* New York Anchor Book, Doubledav and Co. Inc. 1966.

Finnegan, Ruth. *Oral literature in Africa.* Oxford; Clarendon, 1970.

- - -. *Limba Stories and Story Telling.* Oxford: Clarrendon, 1967.

Lord, Albert. *The Singer of Tales.* Anthenaum: 1960. Malinowski, Bronislaw. 'Myths in Primitive Psychology,' in Magic Science and other Science Gbencoe Press, 1948.

Nketia, J. H. *The Music of Africa.* New York: W. W. Norton, 1974.

Okpewho, Isidore, ed. *Oral Performance in Africa.* Ibadan: Spectrum Books Ltd,1990.

Sorell, Walter. *The Dance Through the Ages.* New York: Groset and Dunlap, 1967.

Sekoni, Ropo. "The Narrator, Narrative, Pattern and Audience Experience of Oral Narrative Performance." *Oral Performance in*

Africa. Ed. Isidore Okpewho. Ibadan: Spectrum Books Ltd., 1990. 139 - 159.

Chapter Seven
Riddles and Bash

Notes and References

1.Children of Alaa (or popularly Umuala) are part of a larger autonomous community, in Umuahia South local government of

2.Nigeria's Abia State. They are believed to be offspring of one father called Alaa. Alaa himself was one of the many sons who emigrated some nine hundred metres from Itu with wives and children to the present location. Alaa's motive of migration was uncertain, but is believed to have been due to the usual land disputes and the need for expansion.

2.Oldest living member of Alaa community.

3.Local bard from a lineage of master-performers.

4.There could someday be a computer program for riddle games with visual animations to provide a whole new breath of fresh air from the western junk that dominate the African market. But that would be when African nations have learnt to take cultural dynamics more seriously than the penchant to simply assimilate whatever the western world throws at them with little or no regard for their genuine needs and sensitivity.

Works Cited

Abdulkadir, Dandatti. 'Oral Composition: A Historical Appraisal.' *Oral Poetry of Nigeria.* Ed. E. Abalogu, *Nigeria Magazine* Lagos, 1981. p. 30

don John, Interviews, Alaa, August 1986.

de Joe, Interviews, Alaa, August 1986.

Hagler, Iyorwuere. 'Performance in Oral Poetry.' *Oral Poetry of Nigeria. Nigeria Magazine*, 1981, p. 37

Hymes, Dell. 'The Concept of Performance.' *Oral Poetry.* Calabar, March 1986.

de Joe, Interviews.

de Joe, Interviews.

de Graft, J. C. 'Roots in African Drama and Theatre.' *African Literature Today*, No. 8. New York p. 10.

Abdulkadir, Dandatti p.20.

Egudu, Romanus. 'Oral Poetry.' *Introduction to African Literature*. Ed. U. Beier, London, Longman, 1979 p. 57.

Parry, Milman. Dandatti Abdulkadir. "Oral Composition: A Historical Appraisal," p. 18.

Azuonye, Chukwuma. 'The Formulaic Character of the Oral Epic Songs of the Ohafia-Igbo.' A paper presented at the second International seminar in Igbo Literature, University of Nigeria, Nsukka, August, 1981, p.2.

Azuonye, Chukwuma. p. 3.

Finnegan, Ruth. *Oral Literature in Africa*. London: Oxford University Press, 1970. p.30.

Africa in Narratives

OUR *Africa in Narratives* critical
volume further illuminates or proves,
against the backdrop of attitudes toward
nations deemed "ethnic minorities," that
literature in Africa has lived up to the
challenge of esthetic imagination to form
an active, refreshing part of world
cultural discourse.

Now we can commonly agree that
African literature must continue to reflect
the distinctive imaginative landscape of
that continent defined by its collective
colonial and unique national experience
which, in trend and development, offers a
comparative opposition to the literary
movements of most of the western world.

However current readings seem to
prove that until African countries have
evolved imaginatively beyond their
present ephemeral stages of social and
political turmoil, not to talk of
intellectual imitations of western
thought, national literatures should be
subject to the imperative of a continental
–and hopefully intercontinental–
cooperation.

This conscious understanding, or the
continuous reassessment of heritage, is
borne from the vision which some of
Africa's great founding fathers and
thought leaders had so selflessly, and
also courageously, espoused.

African Library of Critical Writing

SMITH AND CE [ED]

AFRICA
IN
NARRATIVES

Liberian professor of
African languages and
literature, founder of the
Society of African Folklore,
and Literary Society
International, LSi, Charles
Smith, is editor of the
Critical Writing Series on
African Literature with
Nigerian Chin Ce, books,
news, reviews editor and
research and creative writer.
As one of the younger stream
of poets from Africa, Ce is
also the author of several
works of fiction and essays
on African and Caribbean
literature.

African Books Network

AFRICAN Books Network with its cosmopolitan outlook is poised to meet the book needs of African generations in times to come. Since the year 2000 when we joined the highway of online solutions in publishing and distribution, our African alliance to global information development excels in spite of challenges in the region. Our select projects have given boost to the renaissance of a whole generation of dynamic literature. In our wake is the harvest of titles that have become important referrals in contemporary literary studies. With print issues followed by eContent and eBook versions, our network has demonstrated its commitment to the vision of a continent bound to a common heritage. This universal publishing outlook is further evidenced by our participation in African Literature Research projects. For everyone on deck, a hands-on interactive is the deal which continues to translate to more flexibility in line with global trends ensuring that African writers are part of the information gobalisation of the present.

As one of Africa's mainstream book publishing and distribution networks, many authors may look to us for to privileged assistance regarding affiliate international and local publishing and distribution service